10666707

.004

∞

Comfort for
the Sick and Dying

David L. Greenstock

Comfort for
the Sick and Dying

And for Those Who Love Them

Sophia Institute Press®
Manchester, New Hampshire

Comfort for the Sick and Dying: And for Those Who Love Them was first published in 1956 by Newman Press, Westminster, Maryland, under the title *Death: The Glorious Adventure*. This 1999 edition by Sophia Institute Press contains minor editorial revisions to the original text.

Copyright © 1999 Sophia Institute Press®
Printed in the United States of America
All rights reserved
Jacket design by Lorraine Bilodeau

The cover painting is a detail of Carl Heinrich Bloch's
Christ the Consolater (photo couresy of SuperStock).

No part of this book may be reproduced, stored in a retrieval system, or transmitted in any form, or by any means, electronic, mechanical, photocopying, or otherwise, without the prior written permission of the publisher, except by a reviewer, who may quote brief passages in a review.

Sophia Institute Press®
Box 5284, Manchester, NH 03108
1-800-888-9344
www.sophiainstitute.com

Nihil Obstat: John M. T. Barton, S.T.D., L.S.S., *Censor Deputatus*
Imprimatur: E. Morrogh Bernard, *Vicarius Generalis*
Westminster, September 17, 1955

Library of Congress Cataloging-in-Publication Data

Greenstock, David L.
      Comfort for the sick and dying : and for those who
    love them / David L. Greenstock.
        p.   cm.
      Rev. ed. of: Death, 1956.
      ISBN 0-918477-96-4 (pbk. : alk. paper)
      1. Death — Religious aspects — Catholic Church.
    2. Bereavement — Religious aspects — Catholic Church.
    3. Spiritual life — Catholic Church. 4. Future life —
    Catholic Church. I. Greenstock, David L. Death. II. Title.
    BT825.G66   1999
    236 — dc21   99-22614 CIP

99 00 01 02 03 10 9 8 7 6 5 4 3 2 1

Contents

Editor's Note: The biblical references in the following pages are based on the Douay-Rheims edition of the Old and New Testaments. Where applicable, quotations have been cross-referenced with the differing numeration in the Revised Standard Version, using the following symbol: (RSV =).

∽

Foreword

∞

This book is written especially for those who are sick or in danger of death. However, it may also be useful to others who at the moment are in perfect health, because we never know when God is going to demand from us an account of our stewardship. Its main purpose is to explain in simple language those great truths of our Faith which alone can help us when we find ourselves face-to-face with the only reality — God.

Just as it is natural that we should be afraid of death, so also it is equally natural that we should be prepared for it. There is no real need for us to be afraid of it, provided we are ready to meditate on God's mercy toward sinners and to consider the means which He has given us to prepare for the next life.

Comfort for the Sick and Dying

All suffering comes to us from the hands of a God who loves us above all things. He does not will pain for its own sake, but because He knows that good can come of it. It is hoped that this book will bring some consolation to those who are sick and will enable them to unite their sufferings with those of the crucified Christ in such a way that they may be perfectly prepared to see God face-to-face when the moment comes. Christ has conquered death, and we can conquer it, too, if we follow His example and use the means which He has given us.

∞

*Comfort for
the Sick and Dying*

Chapter One

∞

Death is the gateway to eternal life

∞

One of the fundamental instincts of man is self-preservation. It is natural that we should cling to life, because God has given it to us and it is a good thing. At the same time, we know that death is inevitable. The evidence is all around us, and although we may try to ignore it because we do not like to think about it, nevertheless it intrudes upon our thoughts from time to time. The day will come when this life ceases for us and a new life begins. From the physical point of view, we are aware of death and we know what it means. The soul is withdrawn from the body to which it has given movement, sensation, and life. This dissolution may be gradual or sudden, it may come in youth or in old age, and it may be more or less painful, but it is inevitable. It is a law of nature as inexorable as any of her other laws, and like so many others before us, we, too, shall have to submit to it.

Fear of death is natural

Faced with this reality, we are afraid, and to a certain extent, it is natural that we should be, in spite of the fact that we have been raised by God above the natural level and placed, through His mercy, on a divine plane. A closer examination of this fear of death shows us that it is a complex thing. There is an unknown quantity about death which frightens us — we know so little about the life of a soul separated from the body. It is hard for us to imagine an existence without bodily sensations, a life in which sight, touch, taste, smell, and hearing are denied to us. We have no experience of the life of a pure spirit, and the unknown and unexperienced are always frightening.

However, that is not all. As Catholics we are aware of our obligations toward God, and we have some idea, however vague, of the gap between the creature and the Creator. Death means the end of this life, but it also means the beginning of a new life, and there is an examination to be passed before we can take up our new existence. "It is appointed unto man once to die and after death the judgment."[1] If we examine our fear of death, we shall find that it is centered on this fact. All our thoughts, words, deeds, and omissions will be passed in review, and the result will decide the issue — either a life with God for all eternity or a life without Him. When we think of God's majesty and our own weakness, we are afraid — and small wonder.

Then, too, in spite of all its difficulties, our life on this earth has not been without its pleasures. We have enjoyed it, even though it has been interlaced with sorrow and pain. We know it so well: its routine, its surprises, its pleasures. In fact, we have thought rather too much of it, as if it were the only enduring thing we had to grasp hold of, instead of being a transitory

[1] Heb. 9:27.

pleasure, a means to higher things. Now we have to leave it, and with it our friends, our possessions, our interests, and our responsibilities. It is not easy, because not only have those things become familiar companions, but through our mistaken ideas about them, they have also become an essential element in our well-being. Death seems such a final break with all that we have known and loved. We hate the thought of it, and we are afraid of the reality.

It is important to prepare for death

Yet, in spite of all this, if we are wise, we shall not shrink from the thought of death. The very fact that it is inevitable should make us take pains to prepare for it while we have time. After all, we know enough about it to realize that it is the most important thing we shall ever do in this life and that an eternity depends on the manner in which we do it. Indeed, a closer study of it may reveal factors which modify, if they do not altogether remove, our excessive fear of it.

Undoubtedly, this idea of preparing for death is present to the minds of all Catholics worthy of the name, even though they may tend to put it off until another occasion. We all mean to die as well as we can when the moment comes, but in our heart of hearts, most of us feel that we still have plenty of time. Yet, experience — and our Lord's stern warnings — point to the fact that we simply do not know when we shall die. God has hidden from us the time, place, and circumstances of our death. Therefore, there is only one safe course open to us — namely, to make our preparation now, not merely by adopting the correct attitude of mind toward death, but also by making quite sure that we understand the full import and purpose of this life.

Perhaps the greatest danger we all have to overcome is the temptation not to face up to reality. When we were little children, we spent a good deal of our time in beautiful, imaginary worlds which we made for ourselves. Those worlds were full of exciting adventures and strange people. There were struggles against bandits, fights with dragons, and exciting voyages with pirates or as explorers. It was all very entertaining — but it was not life. When we grew older, we realized this to a certain extent as the world of stern reality began to intrude more and more upon our dreams. We did not like it at first, because it implied responsibility, but it was inevitable, and so we accepted it. We may still have indulged in daydreams from time to time, but it became more and more obvious that we could not escape from the reality of life. But did we ever fully understand what the reality of this life implied?

As Catholics we began to perceive dimly at least that this present life is only a preparation for a fuller and more perfect life to come, but I doubt if many of us realized that we were still playing at bandits to a great extent. We grasped this life so firmly that there was grave danger of its becoming the most important thing of all to us, while the fuller life of eternity was pushed into the background.

Death is the gateway to eternal life

This is true of all of us, and our first step in preparing for death must be a reorientation of our ideas, a slow process of forcing ourselves to realize that here we have no abiding city.[2] God has made us for Himself, and no created thing can ever really supply the demands of the human heart for happiness. God made us for an eternal destiny, and if we fail to achieve that, then all our success and happiness on this earth will count for nothing, and our lives will be truly lost. If we fail to attain God in the next life, then it can be said of us as it was of Judas, "It were better for that man had he not been born."[3]

This life is only transitory

It is difficult for us to understand that the things we see around us now so clearly are only transitory. Yet the very fact of death brings it home to us, while

[2] Cf. Heb. 13:14.
[3] Mark 14:21.

Comfort for the Sick and Dying

God Himself tries to teach us this lesson by taking away from us now and again the thing or person we have loved in His place. While we live in this world, we are expected to use the visible things we see around us as means to attain to God — not as ends in themselves.

That is by no means an easy task. Man is by nature selfish and possessive. He must have and own, as if he were their lord and master, those things that have been merely lent to him by God for a time. Yes, of all the lessons we have to learn, this is undoubtedly the most difficult. Above all, we must learn that we do not even possess ourselves. We are not the masters of our own lives but belong to God, soul and body. We shall fulfill our eternal destiny only when we understand this and act on it — when we give Him our minds, our hearts, and our wills in humble submission to His divine will.

That is what we mean when we talk about a Christian life. It is a life that is led for God, not for ourselves — in conformity with His teachings, His commands, and His will rather than with our own. Once we become accustomed to thinking of life in this fashion, we shall not be unduly worried about the physical fact of death, because we will see that it is a moment of transition from one life to another. Perhaps this could be expressed more aptly by saying that death is the end of the journey and the arrival at our destination. The journey has ended, and we are home. Now we can rest and begin our true life. In this way, our first fear, the purely physical fear of death, disappears. Later we shall see how the fear of judgment can be overcome in this life, but for the moment, we must consider more closely the central idea of God's divine purpose in our lives.

When God made man, He planted in him the seeds of greatness by giving him a rational soul which could soar far above the limits of material creation to the realms of ideas and ideals which lie behind it. In His divine mercy, He did far more than this. He gave man, as the one end and purpose of his life, Himself.

Comfort for the Sick and Dying

Man could know God and love Him not merely in this life but in the next, and this knowledge and love would be as perfect as the relationship between crea- ture and Creator would permit. To make this possible, God gave man a new principle of life, sanctifying grace, which alone gives man the power to know and love God as He is in Himself. The purpose of life now be- comes clear. Man must safeguard and develop this gift of grace so that, in the next life, it may come to its full perfection in the vision of God face-to-face. That is the only thing which will fully satisfy man's desire for happiness. To this end all others must be subordinated and related, since life is a unity.

God made you free to love Him

Yet God will not do violence to His own laws or force the wills of His free creatures. He created them free, and free they will remain, even in the face of grace. He is man's only final end, but man, on his part, must act in accordance with his dignity as a free creature. He must choose to attain God freely or to reject Him. God loves man and wishes to be loved by him, but He will not force man's love. From the moment of his creation, nothing except God would ever be able to satisfy fully either the demands of man's mind or the longings of his heart. The whole of his nature was set toward God as a compass is set to the north. If he attains that end, his whole being is satisfied for all eternity, since it has found its full perfection, beyond which nothing can be known or desired.

On the other hand, failure to achieve that end means eternal frustration. Because of his freedom, man can always set up for himself false gods in this life. He can choose some creature and place it on God's throne in his heart — but only for a time. The day will inevitably come when the idol will be overthrown and man's heart will be empty. After death, the purpose of this life will be dreadfully clear to all of us, and from that moment there can be no comfort in creatures unless they have been used as God intended them to be used. If death surprises us at a moment when God does not occupy His rightful place in our lives, we shall be frustrated creatures for all eternity, wanderers without a purpose, torn by hatred for the very creatures we ourselves dared to set upon the throne of God. Through seeking human happiness apart from Him, we shall have lost all claim to peace and happiness for eternity. We shall be twisted, distorted caricatures of what we might have been, had we only taken the trouble to open our eyes to the reality of life in its relation to eternity.

To prepare for death, then, we must prepare to live — to make the divine plan for our lives our own so that we may reach the final perfection of our destiny in accordance with God's plan. This, in turn, implies seeing all things in relation to eternity: valuing them insofar as they are means to that end and rejecting them when they conflict with it. In this way, we shall learn to see death for what it really is: the gateway into life, the end of the journey, and the arrival home.

Chapter Two

∞

Let Christ diminish
your fear of death

∞

Whenever we think of death, behind our minds is the fear of that moment when, stripped of all pretense and self-righteousness, we will stand before God's majesty to be judged. Since this thought is the main cause of our fear of death, any preparation for death must give due consideration to God's judgment.

Being very human, we are all inclined to look at the judgment from our own point of view. To dismiss it as a negligible factor in life would, of course, be stupid. Sin is an outrage against the divine majesty, which, in itself, demands punishment. The more we know about God, the more clearly we see the horror of sin, and the sense of our own guilt may blind us to other factors which are more important. The Devil is well aware of this human failing, and as we approach the moment of death, he does his best to fix all our attention on our own personal sins in such a way as to block from our vision the answer to all sin — the divine love and mercy.

We are not concerned here with those who die in mortal sin, because for them there can be no mercy in the sense of forgiveness. We are thinking rather of those souls who sincerely wish to serve God and to die in His service, but who are afraid of death because they are worried about the punishment for past sins. Are there any thoughts which can, with reason, remove this fear?

∞

God is merciful

We may well thank God every day for revealing to us so clearly the depths of the divine love for all souls and especially for the soul of the sinner. This truth is clear in the Old Testament and still more clear in the New. Indeed, God uses the most dramatic language to bring this great truth home to us. He says that, if the sinner repents, He will no longer remember the sins which have been committed against His majesty;[4] that, even if a mother could forget her children, still He will not forget the souls He has created.[5] We see in the Old Testament the example of David, who admitted his sin against God, and at that very moment the prophet told him that it had been forgiven.[6]

In the New Testament, the law of love reaches its heights. God deigns to become man, to live on this earth, and to die for sinners.

During His life, our Lord taught us by every possible means that He loves the sinner and that He came deliberately to save him from his sin: "I am not come to call the just, but sinners."[7] He describes Himself as the good shepherd who gives his life for his sheep,

---

[4] Cf. Isa. 43:25.
[5] Cf. Isa. 49:15.
[6] 2 Kings 12:13 (RSV = 2 Sam. 12:13).
[7] Matt. 9:13.

who goes in search of the one which is lost and, when he finds it, carries it home on his shoulders rejoicing.[8] Above all, He protests that He will never reject anyone who comes to Him for help: "Him that cometh to me I will not cast out."[9]

By His actions, He showed Himself to be the special friend of all those who were helpless and in sorrow — especially of those who were in sin. The stories of Mary Magdalen[10] and of the woman taken in adultery[11] should make us realize the great pity of the Heart of Jesus for sinners.

As He was then, so He is now. His love can be summed up in the story of the thief on the cross beside Him. He asked for so little, knowing his own guilt, and he obtained so much — an eternity of happiness. "Master, remember me when Thou comest

[8] Cf. Matt. 18:12.
[9] John 6:37.
[10] Cf. Luke 7:37-48.
[11] Cf. John 8:3-11.

into Thy kingdom." "This day thou shalt be with me in Paradise."[12]

This same Jesus is our judge when we die, for God has delivered all judgment into His hands, those hands which still bear the marks of the nails. Can we doubt that He will have mercy on us if we ask Him for it during this time of preparation for death and the judgment?

When we think about that judgment, we should think of Jesus, whose love for us was so great that He died for us. We can be quite sure that He will not allow so great a love to be frustrated by any lack of effort on His part.

He has told us that whatever we ask the Father in His name will be granted, and He has told us to ask with confidence: "Ask and you shall receive; seek and you shall find; knock and it shall be opened to you."[13]

[12] Luke 23:42-43.
[13] Cf. Matt. 7:7.

We have only to go to Him with confidence, and His love will do the rest.

∞

Confession diminishes the fear of judgment

There is no sin so grievous that it cannot be forgiven in this life. This brings us to another thought which can help us to prepare in the right way for death. Our deepest fear, the one that really worries us, is the thought of the judgment to follow after death. Now, God, in His great mercy, has given us an easy means of anticipating that judgment. He has given us the sacrament of Penance.

Penance is a sacrament of judgment. There we appear at the court of divine justice, and we accuse ourselves of our sins (we do not wait to be accused) to a priest who is in the place of Christ, with His divine authority to forgive us. Every time we go to Confession, we anticipate that final judgment at the moment of death, and, if we sincerely repent of the sins we confess, they are removed from our lives forever. No longer will they be mentioned against us; rather they will redound to our glory insofar as they have been pardoned through the merits of the Precious Blood of Christ.

The sacrament of Penance can, and indeed should, be one of the most important factors in our preparation for death. In comparison with the judgment of God, it is such an easy way of freeing ourselves from the burden of our sins. If Christ is merciful to all who call upon Him, He will be still more merciful to one who humbly kneels at His feet and with sincere sorrow confesses his offenses against the divine majesty. "Go, sin no more,"[14] He will say to us — and that is the password to true freedom from fear.

You must trust in Christ's promises

"But," you may say, "there still remains the uncertainty of the next life." That is true in a sense. We

[14] John 8:11.

know so little about the conditions of that life, because we have no experience on this earth which can truly be compared with it, unless, of course, we are in the heights of sanctity. We ordinary folk are very near the earth in many ways, and the things of sense are so very important to us. In our weakness, we forget one thing which is of supreme importance — namely, that someone who has actually experienced death has returned to life and has told us certain things which should console us and help us not to fear it too much. That someone is our Lord Himself.

He rose from the dead as the "firstfruits of them that sleep,"[15] as the first in the long line of those who would imitate His Resurrection, as the living model of our own glorious resurrection if we are faithful to Him. His return to life is the living pledge that one day, we, too, shall experience that reunion of soul and body. As His triumph over death was complete, so shall ours be.

[15] 1 Cor. 15:20.

Still more important perhaps, at least from the point of view of our uncertainty about the next life, are the teachings of Christ. To those who remain faithful to Him, He promised the kingdom of Heaven: "And I dispose to you, as my Father hath disposed to me, a kingdom, that you may eat and drink at my table in my kingdom."[16] He told us that in His Father's house there are many mansions and that He would die and ascend into Heaven to prepare a place for us.[17] He will come from Heaven to greet us at the moment of our death and will take us to Himself that we may be with Him.

At the most solemn moment of His life, just before His agony in the garden, which marked the beginning of His Passion, He prayed to His Father in Heaven for the Church, for His Apostles, and for us. Toward the end of that prayer He said, "Father, I will that where I

---

[16] Luke 22:29-30.
[17] John 14:2-3.

am, they also whom Thou hast given me may be with me; that they may see my glory which Thou hast given me, because Thou hast loved me before the creation of the world."[18] That is His will for us: that we may take our place by His side in Heaven. And because He is the Son of God, no effort on His part will be wanting to bring about that reunion between Him and us.

In view of these thoughts, does it matter very much if we do not know all the minute details of the future life after death? We do know that, waiting for us, is Infinite Love — a God who loves us more than we deserve and also more than we could ever imagine in our wildest dreams. Can we not safely confide our souls into His loving hands and leave them there, safe in the thought that He will look after us? This is all He asks: that we trust Him with the same simplicity with which a child trusts his father. If we do have this

[18] John 17:24.

confidence in Him, we can be sure that He will never let us down, because His own promises — we might say, His very reputation — are at stake.

When He calls us from this world we must go to Him, not as Peter walked on the waters, in fear and trembling,[19] but with great confidence in His infinite love for each soul He has created. True love casts out fear.[20] In this way, the certainty of what awaits us cancels out the uncertainty; we are certain of the most important things, while our ignorance is merely concerned with trifles which need not really worry us.

We can now see more clearly the general lines of our preparation for death. First of all, we must learn to develop a correct mental approach toward this life and its purpose. Realizing that death is the most important thing we shall ever do and that everything depends on

[19] Cf. Matt. 14:29-30.
[20] Cf. 1 John 4:18.

the manner in which we do it, we shall also try to put ourselves in the right frame of mind to meet it as we ought. For this purpose, we must pay attention to those considerations which serve to dispel our exaggerated fears of death and of the judgment which follows it. We must think of those things which lead us to have great confidence in God's mercy, in His love, and in His promises made to us through His Son. Above all, perhaps, we must make good use of the sacrament of Penance, by means of which we can anticipate the judgment by accusing ourselves here and now of our sins and obtaining forgiveness for them.

In a word, sin must go from our lives, to be replaced by real love and confidence. Once we learn to love our Lord enough, we shall cease to be afraid. We are fully aware of this where our earthly loves are concerned; why, then, do we doubt the validity of the same principle when it is applied to the infinite love of God for us? We would trust our parents or our dearest friends with our very lives. Can we not so trust

God, who loves us with an infinitely greater love
than theirs? This, as we shall have occasion to observe
later, is the real secret of dying well. Blindly, without
doubt or hesitation, we must place our lives in God's
hands, accepting His will for us because it is the will
of Him who loves us and to whom we belong
entirely.

Mary will help you prepare for death

Under God, the person who can best prepare us to
die with this complete confidence is our Blessed Lady.
Part of our preparation should consist in a deep personal devotion to her as our mother, together with
constant prayers for her intercession and mediation
under those consoling titles by which the Church
invokes her aid.

If our earthly mothers were canonized by the
Church, imagine with what devotion and confidence
we would turn to them to help us. Yet that is, in fact,
the true position with regard to our relationship with

Mary, the Mother of God. From the moment she gave her consent to the angel's message,[21] she became, not merely the Mother of the Redeemer, but also the mother of the redeemed. Her Son gave her to us in a special way, when she stood at the foot of the Cross, to be our mother also.[22] Like her Son, she, too, passed through the gateway of death into eternal life. Both of them have experienced the separation of soul and body, and both are pledged to help us when we come to the moment of death — Jesus as our Redeemer and Mary as our mother.

When we say the Hail Mary, we ask her to "pray for us sinners, now and at the hour of our death." If we are sincere in our devotion to her, that prayer is sure to be heard.

Consider for a moment of the titles by which the Church invokes her in her litany. She is called the

[21] Cf. Luke 1:38.
[22] Cf. John 19:26.

Mother of Divine Grace, not merely because she is the Mother of our Lord — God's greatest gift to men — but also because God has given into her maternal hands the distribution of all His graces. Among those graces is that of a happy death. She is our mother also, and if we have confidence in her and persevere in our prayers for that favor, she will surely grant it to us through her powerful intercession.

She is the Refuge of Sinners — surely one of her most appealing titles. Her supreme interest has always been the work of her Son. He came to save sinners. Indeed, He showed a special love for them while He was on earth, and His love continues now that He is in Heaven. Mary's interests are identical with His, and therefore, her special care must be for those, of all her children, who are in danger through sin or who are trying hard to avoid sin. When the weight of past or present sin seems too much for us to carry in the light of divine justice, Mary will console us, lead us to greater sorrow and to the love of her Son. As St. Bernard says, it was never known that anyone fled to her protection or implored her help in vain.[23]

She is the Mother of Mercy. She is called this, first of all, because she is the Mother of Christ — and the greatest act of divine mercy was surely the Incarnation. But she deserves this title for another reason. The word *mercy* has lost some of its original meaning in English. It really implies the ability to understand and sympathize with the sufferings of others, together with an active assistance to relieve their distress. The greater the need, the more effective the aid and the greater the compassion. The deepest misery is undoubtedly that of sin; there is no one more unhappy or more lonely than the sinner, since he is out of step with the whole of creation. Our Lord realized this during His life on earth, and Mary understands it only too well. Therefore, her compassionate heart is ever open to the needs of the sinner, and her assistance is ever at hand to help him.

[23] From the prayer the *Memorare*, by St. Bernard (1090-1153), Abbot of Clairvaux.

She knows that the approach of death always brings with it the fear of the judgment, which comes from the consciousness of sin, whether past or present. Her intercession will obtain for us the grace of true repentance for our offenses against her Son. She will encourage us to trust in His mercy, which is infinite, teaching us that true love casts out fear.

We invoke her under the titles of Comfort of the Afflicted and Health of the Sick because the Church understands perfectly her power and her willingness to help those who are in sorrow or who are sick. It is at such times that the temptation to despair makes itself felt, because the Cross is not an easy burden for most of us until we learn to carry it with Jesus.

Often our greatest sorrows come to us when our earthly mothers are no longer with us to console us and to help us with their advice and assistance. God has given us Mary as our heavenly mother. She will take us under her sure protection and will give us the help and advice we need to bear the Cross with patience and as a source of merit. She will teach us the necessity of suffering and show us the part our trials play in the distribution of God's graces to a world in sore need of them. Above all, she will make us realize that all things, pleasant or unpleasant, come to us from the hands of Infinite Love. In the Cross lies our salvation, not merely because Jesus died on the Cross, but also because our own crosses are the surest means to repentance and purification.

Part of our preparation for death should be a deepening of our devotion to Mary, the mother of sinners. In our love for her, we shall find strength and courage to face death because it is God's will for us. Above all, we should ask her frequently and with confidence to obtain for us the grace of final perseverance. Her mother-love will guide us safely home.

Chapter Three
∞

*Suffering can
strengthen your soul*

∞

Atheists have made suffering the keystone of their attempts to prove that God does not exist. How could a good God, such as we claim Him to be, allow His friends to suffer when He is almighty and could prevent it? Even some good Catholics never seem to get near the real answer to this problem, and for all of us, it is a good thing to meditate upon it for a short while. There is no need for us to reply here directly to the atheist, because we know that God exists and that He is infinite goodness. The problem from our present point of view is different. How are we to make the most of suffering, and what motives do we have for accepting with a certain degree of spiritual joy and even consolation the sufferings which God permits in our lives?

∞

Suffering frees you from sin and its penalties

We should never forget that the main cause of suffering is sin. As St. Paul tells us, it was through the disobedience of Adam that suffering and death came into the world.[24] The sin of Adam was not a private affair — it involved the whole human race, since he disobeyed as our head.[25] The penalty falls on all of us. We are born in sin, and we must face the consequences.

Then, too, there are our own individual sins to be taken into consideration. If divine mercy is infinite, so, too, is divine justice, and the penalty for our sins must be paid either in this life or in the life to come. The more conscious we become of our sins, the more ready we should be to accept the punishment which they entail, because we should be as jealous of God's honor as He is.

[24] Cf. Rom. 5:12.
[25] Cf. 1 Cor. 15:22.

Through our sufferings, God purifies us in this life, making us more worthy of Heaven, increasing our merits before Him, and thus preparing us for a higher place in Heaven. Our road to eternal glory and happiness is the rough road of suffering. He warned us, "If any man will come after me, let him deny himself, take up his cross, and follow me."[26] We have indeed pledged ourselves at our Baptism to become like our Savior — and if we would share in His triumphal Resurrection and victory over death, we must also be prepared to live a life of trial and sufferings as He did. We can be sure that He will not impose upon us burdens we cannot bear, nor will He leave us without the necessary graces to carry the Cross with profit.

If the thought of past sins worries us, the hard fact of suffering should console us. If we accept the trials and sorrows of this life — no matter what form they may take — because we wish to do God's will, we can

[26] Matt. 16:24.

be quite sure that every pain we suffer frees us more and more from sin and its penalties. That is a great source of consolation.

There is, however, yet another reason we should look upon suffering as a great honor and give it its real value. This reason is to be found in the great and consoling doctrine of the Communion of Saints. As Catholics we cannot isolate ourselves, either from our fellowmen on earth, from the great company of the saints in Heaven, or from the souls in Purgatory. It is worth our while to think about this doctrine once again in the light of our sufferings. We shall then see more clearly how they fit into the divine plan.

The faithful departed can help you attain Heaven

The intercession of the saints in Heaven should be a great source of consolation to us. They have attained their reward, but they have by no means forgotten their friends on earth or in Purgatory. Constantly they appeal to God, whom they now see face-to-face, to increase our faith, hope, and love. They know only too well how difficult it is for us at times to tread the dark road of faith. They are aware of the temptations to despair of ever attaining Heaven through the divine mercy, because they, too, have passed through those trials on their way to Heaven. As members of the Mystical Body of Christ,[27] their one aim is to further God's glory and help in the redemptive mission of Christ. They are intensely interested in our eternal salvation, because they see how much God loves us. Therefore, we can be sure that their prayers are always with us. And since they are now in Heaven with God, those prayers have a special value. God will not fail to hear the appeals of His special friends.

Among those saints in Heaven we may have someone especially dear to us — a mother, perhaps, or a father, a brother, son, or daughter. They will not forget

[27] The "Mystical Body of Christ" refers to the collective members of the Church, with Christ as the Head. Cf. 1 Cor. 12:27; Col. 1:18.

us in our hour of need — we can be sure of that. We are destined by God to be one of that glorious company and to take our place with them in Heaven. In a very true sense, we have friends at court on whom we can rely.

Then there are our friends in Purgatory. They love God more intensely than the greatest saint on earth could ever love Him. They know how much they are in debt to us for our prayers for them, our Masses, and the indulgences we have gained for them, and they are eager to pay that debt. They cannot help themselves, because the time for merit has passed, but they can help us. Since they love God so much, they, too, are anxious to bring to Heaven the souls He loves so dearly and for whom He died on the Cross. Their prayers will be joined to those of the saints in Heaven on our behalf, because they, too, are fully aware of the difficulties and dangers which sufferings and the fear of death bring in their train. They know how easy it is to fritter away those precious moments of pain which

can do so much to free us from sin's effects on the *Please God!*
soul. Perhaps we also have in Purgatory friends and
relatives whom we loved on earth and for whom we
have offered prayers after their death. We can be sure
that they are now doing all they can for us — and
their prayers are very powerful before God who loves
them so much.

∞

Your sufferings can help the souls in Purgatory

But we, too, are members of that same Mystical
Body, and we must think of our illnesses, sufferings,
and even death itself in the light of that doctrine. If
we are helped by the prayers of the saints in Heaven
and of the souls in Purgatory, we also have our obligations toward them. We have our part to play in the
redemptive mission of Christ on earth. All these
obligations can be perfectly fulfilled by means of our
illness and sufferings, if we wish it.

To accept suffering as a gift from the hands of God
and to embrace it because it is His divine will implies

not merely great love of God, but also the exercise of the virtue of religion. It is a true prayer made, not with the lips, but with our bodies joined to our wills. Such an act of virtue brings joy to the saints in Heaven, because they know how much it means in terms of personal merit for ourselves and glory given to God. It makes us very like Christ, our model, who suffered all things because it was the will of His Father in Heaven.

At the same time, our sufferings, accepted and offered to God for the souls in Purgatory, bring them great relief and place them even more in our debt than they were before. Nothing is more pleasing to God than an act of charity performed on behalf of these souls. They, too, are suffering, and if we can aid them by our pain on earth, we can be sure that God will reward us beyond measure for our charity and selflessness.

We must learn to realize the immense value of our sufferings in terms of help given to others on earth. Suffering properly endured is the most powerful prayer we shall ever make to God, not merely for ourselves, but also for others. He has conditioned many of His graces on the prayers of the members of His Mystical Body. The conversion of some poor pagan whom I have never seen, the healing of the wounds of sin in some soul, the grace of salvation for another — all these may easily depend on me, helpless on a bed of pain. Am I going to refuse to help in that divine mission, or am I going to play my part as a faithful member of the Body of Christ? For these reasons, every moment of my illness or suffering is something precious in the sight of God.

We did not choose to be ill or in pain — it was God who allowed us to suffer. When we accept such pain, we are accepting the divine will for us at that moment, and that in itself is a magnificent prayer. There is so much we can do with these sufferings, and the needs of the Church are very great. For this reason alone, it is important for us to have the right attitude toward suffering and to accept it from the hands of

God as a special token of His love. He lays the Cross most heavily on His special friends.

∞

Suffering allows you to become like Christ

But why should God, who loves us, wish us to suffer at all? To understand something of this mystery of pain, we must return to a deeper consideration of Christ, our model. He came to earth to suffer, to become the Man of Sorrows[28] — in a word, to carry the Cross. But it was not really His Cross; it was mine and yours. He came to pay the full price for our sins, not for His own, because He was sinless. In return for our disobedience, He gave to His Father full and perfect obedience in all things.

The whole idea of our lives as Christians is to become like Him. He is our Head, and we are His members. Therefore, we cannot really expect any other treatment than that which was given to Him. If we

[28] Isa. 53:3.

wish to be like Him, if we wish to share in His triumphal Resurrection, we must also be willing to accompany Him through His Passion and death. The Cross is our inheritance, but it is also our glory. We shall never be so like Him in all our lives as when we are suffering in union with Him. It is not the mere fact of suffering which counts; it is suffering with Christ — a joining of our redemptive efforts with His. Then we share in some mysterious fashion in His own divine mission of redemption through pain. This is our great opportunity to forget self and to plunge that self into the Godhead from which it came at the moment of its creation.

∞

Suffering helps you to become selfless

Our great enemy is self-love; we know that from bitter experience. It lies at the root of all our sins, whether mortal or venial, and is responsible for all our failures to cooperate with God's graces. When God lays the cross of suffering upon us, that self-love will raise many objections. It may even attempt to extract a certain amount of pleasure from illness, demanding from those around us absolute service at our beck and call and objecting when they do not attend to us as we would like. It will certainly demand sympathy and consolations. These weaken the power for good which is latent in our sufferings.

On the other hand, we can, if we will it, destroy the power of self through our suffering. We can accept the pain as our due, knowing that we have deserved far more than this as punishment for our sins. Pain can bring us on our knees before God as nothing else can. It can bring home to us our nothingness and our dependence on Him. Above all, it can make us humbly readjust our sense of values. How careful we have always been to look after our bodily comforts, sometimes perhaps at the expense of our spiritual well-being. Now God has put these two in their right proportions before our minds. We can at least accept that and make sure that self now gives place to the glory of God.

Suffering can strengthen your soul

The efforts we make to use our sufferings for the good of others, whether in Purgatory or on earth, will gradually make us forget self and be more considerate for those who have to look after us in times of sickness. We will not make extraordinary demands on their time or patience; rather, we will glorify God, who has given us some measure of comfort and relief from pain through their efforts. And we will not demand sympathy and consolations from them as our right. On the contrary, we shall admit that we have deserved all this and more by our sins. All this will diminish the demands which self makes upon us during illness and will bring us into ever closer union with God and especially with Christ, our model of suffering.

If we choose to make it so, this illness can be the greatest act of love we have ever performed for God. It can make us saints. Not only will it deepen our faith, but it will also give us many opportunities for calling on God in loving confidence, willing to place our lives in His hands and leave them there. We shall never pray better than in and through our sufferings and our willing acceptance of them because they are God's will for us here and now. Nor will our prayer ever be so selfless, so concentrated on adoration of God, and, for that very reason, so effective.

Indeed, suffering is a golden opportunity to wipe away all the mistakes and the sins of the past, and to take our rightful place in the Mystical Body of Christ. The power of a soul which is suffering is truly immense before God, but only if that suffering is accepted as God's will. It is not the mere fact of pain and suffering which is so powerful for good; it is the fact that we are willing to be obedient to the will of God even unto death if necessary. We can thus play our full part in the redemptive work of Christ by joining our will to His in perfect obedience. That is the highest form of love and one which cannot fail to lead us to God.

Chapter Four

*Let Christ's redemptive
sacrifice be your example
and your strength*

Our Lord redeemed us by His willing acceptance of suffering and death in absolute obedience to the will of His Father. The history of His Passion as recorded for us by the evangelists paints a vivid picture of what that Redemption cost Him in terms of suffering. The main incidents in it are so well known that it is useful to think them over again from time to time, so as not to take them for granted.

Christ has endured all your sufferings

All types of suffering are represented in the story of the Passion. We see the mental agony in the garden, when fear of physical pain, combined with the knowledge of the many souls who would reject His sacrifice in spite of all it cost Him, made His sweat pour out as drops of blood.[29] Yet, He accepted it willingly as His Father's will. We can learn a great deal from His prayer: "Father, if it be possible, let this chalice pass from me, but not my will, but Thine be done."[30]

He suffered desertion and betrayal too, and both must have wounded Him still more deeply, because they came to Him through His friends. Only once do we find a complaint wrung from His lips during the whole Passion. It happened in the garden, or just outside it, when Judas came up to Him and, as a sign of identification, saluted Him with a kiss. That was almost too much for the Heart which loved Judas so much in spite of his sin. "Dost thou betray the Son of Man with a kiss?"[31] He asked, as if to say, "Will you use the very sign of intimate love and friendship to betray me?"

[29] Luke 22:44.
[30] Cf. Matt. 26:39; Luke 22:42.
[31] Luke 22:48.

It is clear how much these mental sufferings hurt Christ in His human nature. But there was more to come. He was rejected by His chosen people — the Jewish nation, which had received so many great favors from God and which was the cradle of the Savior of the world. "His blood be upon us and upon our children."[32] He was accused of blasphemy — He who was the Son of God.[33] They mocked Him up to the last few moments of His life, telling Him that they would believe in Him if He would only come down from the Cross.[34]

Again, we might consider His physical sufferings, the scourging which left no part of His sacred flesh without its wounds; the dreadful crowning with thorns; the tiring journey to Calvary; the physical pain of the nailing to the Cross — and then the long, cramping agony for three hours. Yet His very first words from that Cross were to plead for mercy for those who had

[32] Matt. 27:25.
[33] Matt. 26:65.
[34] Matt. 27:42.

rejected and crucified Him: "Father, forgive them, for they know not what they do."[35]

When we come to the end of the dreadful scene, the picture changes. Crucifixion was a slow death from cramp and suffocation due to the gradual infiltration of blood into the lungs. Usually those who died in this fashion could not speak toward the end; but it was not so with Christ. He cried out with a loud voice to His heavenly Father and gave up His life with joy in His heart, because the redemptive sacrifice was now accomplished and sinful man was free forever from the bonds of sin and death. Truly this last scene is not one of sorrow but of triumph — the victory of supreme love over petty hate and sin.

In our preparation for death, we should not ignore the Passion of our Lord. It will give us great strength, because it will teach us, as nothing else can, the power of love to overcome suffering in joy. If He could suffer

[35] Luke 23:34.

so much for us, then we can accept our pain in union with Him for the salvation of the world. We can even accept death from the hands which were nailed to the Cross for us, because we know that our Lord has already passed through that experience and that He knows what it means to die willingly in union with the divine will. God expressed His great love for us in the form of suffering because it is the supreme test of love. We can do the same for Him in a small way because we love Him.

Christ has set up His Cross between Heaven and earth as a living testimony to the fact that the sure way to union with God is through the divine crucible of pain. When we suffer, we are one with Christ, and in our pain God sees the wounds of His Son crying to Heaven for pardon for the sins of men.

∞

The Mass prepares you for death

Yet that is not all, because we can unite ourselves every day of our lives with Christ's death on the Cross in the sacrifice of the Mass. By this means, we prepare ourselves perfectly for a ready acceptance of God's will at the moment of death. In that light, let us examine for a few moments our part in the Mass.

As we know, the Mass is the greatest prayer we shall ever offer, because it is the prayer of Christ's eternal intercession for us through His death. At Mass, the Church takes into her hands the crucified Savior and offers Him once more as a living Victim to God. Being present at Mass, we are present at Calvary, and His sacrifice becomes ours in a special way. Just as the thought of Christ's Passion can be of great use to us in preparing for suffering and death, so, too, can the sacrifice of the Mass be a great source of comfort and strength when that time comes.

However, much will depend on the use we have made of the Mass during life. We can either take our place at the foot of the Cross in the spirit of Mary and St. John, or we can be idle spectators. It depends on us.

Christ's redemptive sacrifice

When we go to Mass, then, let us first of all fix our attention on what we are about to do. We are not to be idle spectators at the sacrifice; we have an active part to play in it. Together with the priest, we offer this sacrifice to God in the name of the whole Church in adoration of His divine majesty, thanking Him for all His benefits and pleading for forgiveness of sin and for those graces which we need for soul and body. Our part in the Mass is essential and vital; it is active, not merely passive. The Church reminds us of this during the Mass itself. The priest identifies us with himself when he turns to us and says, "Pray, brethren, that our sacrifice may be acceptable to God the Father."

In what, then, does this active share in the Mass consist? Primarily, of course, in the fact that we, as members of the Mystical Body, are joined together in a common act of worship, in which we offer to God the sacrifice of His Son. Calvary is, as it were, placed in our hands at that moment, so that we may perform an act of adoration worthy of the Church of Christ.

And that is not all. As living members of His Body, we need help and sanctification to be more worthy of Him. In the Mass, He has given us His own sacrifice to plead with God for all that we need.

Our great obstacle to union with God is sin. Through the Mass, we can destroy sin in our souls by obtaining from God the gift of sincere contrition and an ever-increasing union with Him by grace. We have already stressed the fact that union with Christ should be the mainspring of our lives. It was to this that we dedicated ourselves at Baptism, and it is toward this union that all our sufferings and death itself are directed. Therefore, by increasing that union with Christ through the Mass, we prepare ourselves to accept from God's hands both suffering and death as the gateway to perfect union with our Lord in Heaven.

At the same time, the Mass is a great source of grace, since it is the most perfect prayer we shall ever offer to God. By means of it, we can fulfill perfectly our religious obligation of worship. This fact, of its very nature, brings us nearer to the perfect adoration of God in Heaven. As our grace increases, so the union of our will with the will of God becomes closer and more effective, and this union of wills is the key to the mystery of suffering.

Now the secret of our active participation in the Mass becomes clearer. We are expected to offer ourselves together with Christ as part of that sacrifice. If we consider for a moment the meaning of sacrifice as an act of worship, we shall see that the idea of identification of the worshipers with the victim runs all through the symbolism of this act. Sacrifice is essentially a symbolic action to express the supreme dependence of man on God. In the higher types of sacrifice, this is denoted by the taking of life, and since man is not allowed to take his own life even to worship God, he selects a victim to represent him. In taking the life of that victim, man expresses his absolute submission to God, the author of all life.

Comfort for the Sick and Dying

This identification of victim and offerers goes even deeper in the case of the Mass, because Christ, the Victim, is identified with the members of His Mystical Body. He is one with them as the head is one with the body. He is ours, and we, in our turn, are His. Consequently, in the very act of sacrifice by which we offer Christ once again to the Father, we are also offering ourselves. Here is the real secret of the Mass as a preparation, not merely for life, but also for death. As Christ lived for God, so we are prepared to live for Him. As Christ suffered and died, so we are willing to accept suffering as a means to greater union with God.

We know that we are sons of God and heirs to the kingdom of Heaven through the merits of Christ's Passion and death. We have indeed been bought with a great price. Therefore, we are prepared to receive the application of that redemption to our souls at whatever price God may place on it in our case. Sufferings and death are the inevitable gateway into eternal life.

We have become partakers in the divine life because Christ first became a sharer in our human nature and, as its representative, gave His life for us. We must therefore be prepared to give our lives for Him. We must be willing to live for Him, to suffer with Him, and to die in union with His death. That is the meaning of our Mass.

The Eucharist assists and sanctifies you

When we think of the Eucharist, not merely as a sacrifice, but also as a sacrament, we reach the same conclusion. Our Lord's gift of Himself in Holy Communion is essentially a life-giving gift. "He that eateth me . . . same also shall live by me."[36] "He that eateth this bread shall live forever"[37] is His promise to those who receive Him worthily. By its very nature, this sacrament is an act of vital union between the soul

[36] John 6:58.
[37] Cf. John 6:52.

and Christ. He is as truly present within us at Holy Communion as He was in the stable at Bethlehem and on the wood of the Cross. That union has one supreme object: to increase the love which exists between us.

If we consider how our Lord does this in Holy Communion, we discover one of the intimate secrets of divine love. Whereas human love is attracted by good qualities which it finds in the object of its affection, divine love is essentially a giving — it produces good in the one it loves. God, in loving me, makes me good. This is true in a special way of the Holy Eucharist. It is an act of supreme divine love that Christ should wish to come to me and dwell in me. Being an act of love, this indwelling tends naturally to increase my goodness. This it does, first of all, by an increase in the sanctifying grace which I already possess, rooting it ever deeper in my soul, and activating it so that it overflows into acts of fervent faith, confidence, and love.

Alternatively, we can think of Holy Communion as an intimate reunion of two friends. In this sacrament, our best friend comes to visit us — and we can be quite sure that He does not come empty-handed. All the treasures of His grace are at our disposal during those moments. He comes to help us to live in very close union with Him in the ordinary circumstances of our daily lives. When those circumstances include sorrow or suffering, we can be even more certain of His help. If He knows that it is good for us and for the Church, He may not remove the sorrow, but He will give us all the strength we need to bear it properly and with spiritual profit for ourselves and for others. In that sense, He will comfort and sustain us in our efforts.

Through this sacrament, the life-giving sap of the True Vine flows through us, its branches.[38] That increase of grace means a corresponding increase in our

[38] John 15:1, 4-5.

perfection and brings us ever nearer to our full perfection in Heaven. He will purify us in this life so that we shall have less suffering in Purgatory. This, although we may not always appreciate it, is a great favor.

In all these senses, then, our Holy Communions are a constant pledge of our final resurrection and future glory in Heaven. "He that eateth this bread shall live forever" was our Lord's promise, and He will keep His word.

From this it follows that, if we approach this sacrament in the right dispositions, it can be a constant, steady preparation for sickness, sorrow, and death, because it is a preparation for eternal life. We owe a special debt to the Holy Father for His recent decree on Holy Communion.[39] He has made it easier for us to approach the altar more frequently, and we should do all

[39] In his Apostolic Constitution *Christus Dominus* (January 16, 1953), Pope Pius XII standardized the relaxations in the Eucharistic fast that had been introduced during World War II. — ED.

we can to take advantage of this. Those who are sick or who feel that they are unable to fast before Holy Communion should consult their confessor to see whether they can obtain relief from their difficulties under this new decree. It is the wish of the Holy Father that all should take advantage of these privileges where necessary in order to receive our Lord frequently. We can always make up for our inability to fast by a more fervent reception of our Lord and by the care with which we thank Him for His wonderful mercy and love.

Chapter Five

The Holy Spirit comforts
those who suffer

∞

One day, perhaps when we were still very young, we knelt in front of the bishop, who placed his hand on our head, anointed us with chrism on the forehead in the form of a cross, and said to us, "I sign thee with the Sign of the Cross, and I confirm thee with the chrism of salvation in the name of the Father and of the Son and of the Holy Spirit." It was the day of our Confirmation. On that day, the Holy Spirit came to us in a special way, as He did to the Apostles on the feast of Pentecost.[40]

To understand more clearly what happened in our souls on that occasion, we must go back in thought to that first Pentecost. Our Lord had ascended into

[40] Acts 2:1-4.

Heaven, after telling the Apostles and disciples that they must wait in Jerusalem until the Holy Spirit should come upon them as He had promised. They had obeyed this command and were all gathered together in prayer in a room of a house in Jerusalem. They were still afraid of what was going to happen to them, and they did not yet fully understand what our Lord expected them to do. Suddenly, there was a sound as of a mighty wind rushing through the house. The room seemed full of little darting flames, which settled over the head of each one of them. At that moment, as the Scripture tells us, they were all filled with the Holy Spirit. He had come to teach them, to guide and strengthen them.

Immediately they went out into the streets of the city, their fear of the chief priests forgotten, and began to preach the doctrine of Christ by their words and by their example. The history of the spread of the Gospel throughout the whole world had begun. They were no longer weak men, but strong in faith and firm of purpose. They were willing to suffer any hardship, even death itself, for the cause of their master.

When we were confirmed, we did not hear the sound of the rushing wind or see the flaming tongues of fire — yet we, too, received the same gift of the Holy Spirit and for the same purpose. After the bishop had imposed his hand on us and anointed us with chrism, we became dedicated to God's service in a special way as soldiers of Christ, willing to fight His battles and to suffer all things to advance His cause. He may not ask us to do this in any spectacular fashion — for example, by martyrdom — but He will certainly demand that we bear witness to Christ in our lives. This implies that we should live, suffer, and die as Christians — not as pagans who have never heard of Christ.

The life of a good Catholic is a living example of the efficacy of the teaching of Christ, so that Christ can say of him, as St. Paul said of his converts in Thessalonica, "From you was spread abroad the word of the Lord . . . in every place; your faith which is toward God is gone forth."[41] The Holy Spirit whom we have received in Confirmation gives us the strength to live good lives in a world which is fast losing all respect for God and for His laws. If we live the Gospel, we preach the Gospel.

∞

The Holy Spirit comforts and strengthens you

When the time comes for us to meet suffering, the same Holy Spirit gives us comfort in our hour of trial and the strength to bear our pain in spite of human weakness. He does this, first of all, by His presence within us. This gift of the indwelling of God in our souls, which comes to us first at Baptism, is increased at Confirmation. We are not, and never can be, alone anymore, provided we live in God's grace. He lives in us and works through us. This is never more true than in our times of sorrow. Then He whom the Church

[41] 1 Thess. 1:8.

calls the Comforter will be with us. Unlike human comfort, God's comfort reaches the very depths of our being, making us realize the value of our sufferings in terms of merit and intercession for the whole Mystical Body. Through His grace, He will allow us to see God's hand in our sufferings and will help us to accept the divine will in humble submission. He will show us that in the acceptance of His will lies our sure road to salvation.

Above all, Confirmation is the sacrament of courage. Just as the Holy Spirit fortified the hearts and minds of the Apostles and the martyrs of the Church, so, too, He will give us the gift of fortitude which will enable us to bear all things, including death itself, for God. Those who are sick know very well the need they have for this gift. In sickness, the bodily resistance is lowered steadily until we can become just one great suffering nerve, feeling the pain more intensely as time goes on. We are no longer capable of helping ourselves and must rely on the good offices of others. To an independent spirit, this can be a great trial. Then, too, those who are in good health do not seem to understand how the slightest thing can increase the burden of sickness. The mind becomes more sensitive, and the emotions are under less direct control.

We know that we should pray — but prayer is an effort when we are sick, and we have yet to learn that the very illness itself, patiently endured for Christ, is perhaps our finest prayer. The Holy Spirit will teach us this truth and will bring it home to us in such a way that we shall find great consolation in our pain. Through His gifts of understanding and wisdom, the Holy Spirit will teach us to see God in our sufferings as perhaps we have never seen Him before in this life.

Think of the names the Church gives to the Holy Spirit in the Pentecost hymn. She calls Him the Father of the Poor — and remember that, in the sight of God, we are all beggars. We have nothing belonging to ourselves except sin. We know from the Old Testament and from the New that the poor are especially dear to God, and by "the poor" we mean the humble of heart. If we humble ourselves under the mighty hand of God, the Holy Spirit will look after us as a father cares for his children. For this reason, the Church also addresses Him as the Giver of Gifts — especially of those graces which we all need when we are in sorrow or sickness.

She also calls Him the Light of Hearts, because only He who is divine truth itself can give us the light to see our sufferings as part of God's plan for the salvation of our own souls and of those of countless others. In that same hymn, we speak of God the Holy Spirit as the Best of All Consolers, the soul's Delightful Guest and a Sweet Refuge in time of distress. These titles are not empty words. God loves us more than any human being can ever love us, and because He loves us, He also has mercy on us and will pity us in our distress. From Him comes that divine, secret consolation which alone can really comfort a soul faced with the terrors of illness and possibly death.

He dwells in us, never leaving us for a moment, as our sure shield against all temptations and as a very dear friend. In His arms we can find refuge and obtain the fulfillment of that promise: "Blessed are they that mourn, for they shall be comforted."[42]

The Holy Spirit perfects you through suffering

The Holy Spirit comes into our souls to perform there His greatest work: the task of our sanctification. God's love is so different from human love, so much more powerful and effective. When all others are powerless to help us, we can safely turn to Him in whose mighty hands lies the whole of creation. He loves all the works of His hands, but above all He loves the soul in which He dwells so intimately through the gifts of His grace. One soul in a state of grace is worth more in the sight of God than all the material creation put together. He has planned great things for that soul,

[42] Matt. 5:5.

and the Holy Spirit will work on it constantly until its sanctification and salvation are assured.

This is true of all the souls for whom Christ died on the Cross; but how much more is it true of those who stand on the threshold of eternity. They suffer, it is true, but they are also very near that great moment when they will be taken home to live forever with the God who loves them. In these circumstances, His special care and protection will go out to those souls. They need Him even more than the others who are still far from their goal; in their case every moment is precious and must be used to the full. The burning flames of divine love must act to the full now in order to purify and perfect those souls for God's greater glory. How great God's efforts must be at that moment can be measured only in terms of the Crucifixion — He was willing to lay down His life for our salvation.

In times of trouble and sickness, we would do well to remember our Confirmation and the great gifts we have received through it. As you know, it is a sacrament which does not need to be repeated; its effects last as long as our life endures. Earnest prayers to God will secure for us at any moment those graces which are our due once we have been consecrated as soldiers of Christ. It will be entirely our own fault if we do not receive them — since they are ours for the asking — or if we do not make the most of them once God has given them to us.

Every day in our prayers we should make acts of love of the Holy Spirit dwelling in our souls, asking Him to help us to live and die as faithful servants of God. Since He desires this grace for us as much as, if not more than, we desire it ourselves, we can be sure that persevering prayer will bring a swift reply in the form of grace to bear our sufferings with patience.

Whenever we feel that our sufferings are too much for us, or in time of temptation, when we feel on the verge of despair, then, once more, we should call to mind this Divine Presence within us. We have Someone with us who loves us with an infinite love

and who can help us at every moment. We have a
Friend whose love is all-embracing and who is also
all-powerful. He will accompany us on our last journey
and will be waiting for us at its end. All He asks is that
we turn to Him and trust Him implicitly. With that
trust, we shall overcome all temptations and win
through safely.

Fear of the Lord diminishes fear of punishment

One of the gifts of the Holy Spirit which will be
of great use to us in times of sickness is fear of the
Lord. This gift enables us to look on God as a loving
Father. It helps us to have genuine sorrow for sin from
the highest motives. It is a common thing, in times of
sickness, to feel afraid of God's justice and of the punishment which we know we have deserved for having
sinned against Him. But we must never allow the fear
of punishment to overshadow or diminish our rever-
ence for God as our Father. We should feel sorrow, not
merely because we are liable to suffer punishment, but

also because our sins have been committed against One who loves us as a father loves his children.

Through the gift of fear of the Lord, we shall draw closer to God as a result of those very sins which have offended Him. Sin — like everything else — has its part to play in the workings of Divine Providence. For one thing, it serves to keep us humble, making us realize that unless we keep very close to God, we shall be lost. Above all, the knowledge of our sins and God's forgiveness of them serves to increase our reverential fear, removing all tepidity and indifference from the performance of our daily duties, especially our prayers. It brings fervor to those daily acts of submission to God's will which in themselves prepare us as nothing else can for sickness and death. Fear is indeed the beginning of wisdom.

We should cultivate a deep personal devotion to the Holy Spirit, the Sanctifier, making our own the sentiments of the Church in her Pentecost hymn. He who brought Christ, the Savior, to the chaste womb of

Mary will also bring Him into our hearts, helping us to stir up within us the great graces which have been given to us at our Confirmation and preparing us ever more perfectly as time goes on for our union with Him in Heaven.

Chapter Six

∞

Christ can bring good out of your suffering

∞

It still surprises many people to read in the Gospel those words of Christ: "My yoke is sweet and my burden light."[43] It would seem that here we are faced with one statement at least that is not strictly true, since suffering is the lot of all who dwell on this earth — and suffering is no light burden. Before we examine in greater detail some practical aspects of sickness, we should consider for a moment the general problem in the light of our Lord's remark. Then we shall be in a better position to determine our attitude toward the difficulties, both physical and spiritual, to which illness gives rise.

The problem of suffering has preoccupied the mind of many from the time of the sin of Adam. We find it

[43] Matt. 11:30.

discussed under various aspects in the Old Testament. The book of Job, for example, is a survey of the problem itself and of the many solutions which have been proposed in reply to it.

God led mankind little by little to the fullness of Revelation in Christ. Therefore it need not surprise us to find that, in the Old Law, the solution to the problem was almost entirely a material one. The just man, no matter what he has to suffer, will triumph in the end. God will bless him with material prosperity if he perseveres. The work of his hands will prosper, he will be blessed with many children, and his life itself will be prolonged. God's answer to the problem as set out in the book of Job is to show by many examples the depth of divine wisdom in comparison with man's very limited knowledge. Man must learn to trust God, who knows what is best for him.

Gradually, as the Old Testament Revelation unfolds itself, the reward of the just man who has to suffer is less material and more spiritual. Man may have to suffer in many ways right up to the end of his life on earth, but the reward for such suffering will come infallibly in the next life if it is endured for God in the right spirit.

Christ has sanctified suffering

With the coming of Christ, however, suffering was — and we may rightly use this word — consecrated. Man was redeemed by suffering motivated by love. It is only in the light of this fact that we catch a glimpse of the true meaning of our Lord's teaching on suffering. Because of His own death on the Cross, He was able to say, "Blessed are they that mourn. . . . Blessed are ye when they shall persecute and calumniate you. . . . My yoke is sweet and my burden light."[44]

In the Old Law, the loss of goods, family, health, and life itself were considered very grave evils. In the New Law of love, we are expected to esteem these

[44] Matt. 5:5, 11; 11:30.

material things less than our spiritual good in this life
and in the next. We are not asked to despise them,
because all things which God has made are good; but
we are expected to keep them in their right proportion.
They are good and useful insofar as they lead us to God
and help us to serve Him in and through them. When
they cease to do that, they also cease to be good — at
least for us.

Sorrow and suffering now take on a new aspect in
the blinding light shed on them from the Cross. Christ's
sufferings were not simply circumstances of our redemption. They are, in a very real sense, *our* sufferings, because, after all, the Cross which He carried was
not His but ours. We have all sinned, either through
Adam or by our own actual sins. In His love for us,
Christ accepted the debt we owe to God as if it were
His own, and He paid it to the full. Lest we should be
mistaken in our estimation of the gravity of sin or of
the extent of God's love for us, He paid that debt with
a wealth of suffering and pain — precious coinage

indeed, if it has won for us God's friendship and an eternity of happiness with Him in Heaven.

From the moment of Christ's Incarnation, a new reality was born into this world, something we call the Mystical Body of Christ. He is the Head of a great family, and we are the members of that family. It is because He is our Head that He was able to redeem us, and it is because we are the members of His Body that we are expected to cooperate in that Redemption. For this reason, we are asked to suffer — not because God likes to see us in pain, but because suffering rightly endured for God is one of the easiest and most profitable methods of making sure of our cooperation with Christ in the mystery of the world's Redemption. It has been well named the sacrament of pain.

Suffering proves and protects love

In the New Testament to which we belong, there is an affinity between suffering and love. It is in this affinity that we shall discover the real meaning of our

Comfort for the Sick and Dying

Lord's words quoted at the beginning of this chapter. If it is love which suffers, then the yoke is sweet and the burden light. This is true in terms of even purely human love. A mother does not care how much she has to suffer, provided the pain brings some relief to the children she loves so much. Indeed, in many cases, love is its own suffering — not the love that is grasping or self-centered, but that which is truly selfless. The acts of self-denial prompted by love are done freely and easily. We long to give presents to those we love, even though it may mean that we have to go without something in order to do it. We give those we love our time, our labor, and our finest efforts. The greater our love for them, the less we count the cost in terms of goods or personal effort. If we count it at all, it will be in terms of love.

The same is true of the love of God, whether we look at it from His point of view or from our own. We know with what joy He went to His death for us; but however much we meditate on that fact, we shall never plumb the depths of that love. If we leave out of consideration the Real Presence in the Blessed Sacrament, there will never be another act of love like it in the whole history of the world. We know it as a fact — to realize it, we shall have to suffer.

In some mysterious fashion, our sufferings are necessary for the good of the whole Mystical Body. It is not merely a question of accepting whatever trials God may choose to send us as a means of expiating our own personal sins, although, of course, our generous acceptance of suffering does, in fact, serve as expiation. There is more to it than that. Our sufferings are a bond of love between us and Christ, since it is part of love's function to desire a share in the sufferings of those we love. Indeed, very often it is this very sharing in the sorrows of others which increases our love for them.

As we increase in God's love, so shall we desire a greater share in His sufferings on the Cross, because by our own pain we can in some measure prove our love for Him and also repay Him for His love. As the measure of our love increases, so, too, will our realization of His divine mission. We shall understand more fully the part we have to play in the application of the fruits of His Redemption. Thus the two elements in the great commandment of love[45] will fuse into one and attain ever-growing harmony. Love for Christ will lead us to accept suffering so that others may receive the grace to love Him more. We shall desire to love Him in our pain to make up for the coldness and indifference of so many others who do not love Him.

It is clear, then, that in the New Law of love, suffering takes its rightful place, not indeed as something good in itself or something in which God delights for its own sake, but as an effective instrument for paying love's debt. It is the great proof of a disinterested, unselfish love, and it is in the light of love alone that suffering can have any meaning.

[45] Matt. 22:37-39.

Christ can bring good out of suffering

∞

Suffering gives opportunities to grow in holiness

It is true, of course, that this desire of love to share in the Passion may not make the sufferings themselves any lighter — on the contrary, it may even increase them. But it does give meaning and texture to the higher purpose of pain, just as, in some mysterious way, it makes the pain easier to bear.

God allows us to suffer because from our pain He draws greater good for ourselves and for others. Only too frequently we would be selfish, merciless creatures were it not for our sufferings. We would be conscious rather of our own ease and comfort than of the miseries and unhappiness of others. In that sense, pain is a great leveler. It leads us to a greater insight into the lives of others; it gives us the words with which to ease their pain and the sympathy necessary to seek out those in trouble in order to help them. Pain teaches us humility when we see the edifice of our pride in our physical or intellectual strength pulled

down to the common level of humanity. Our sense
of prayer increases, because we soon discover that suffering is impossible to bear without union with God.
Also, we learn the great secret that doing the will of
God is always the finest prayer — and nearly always
the hardest. Pain brings about in the soul an effective
adjustment in our sense of values, because we learn
how transient are the things of this world and how
very real are those spiritual realities which we have
so often neglected for more material comforts.

Perhaps voluntary mortification has been neglected
in our lives or at best accepted because imposed on
us by the Church. Now we have to accept mortification from the hands of God. The result is a gradual
purification which can easily lead to great heights of
sanctity. It may even be that occasions of sin have
separated us from God, and that, in His mercy, He
has tied us to a bed of pain in order to break the
chains which have held us in subjection for so long.
Often it is necessary for God to strip us of all that

we previously held so dear in order to make us turn
to Him.

Maybe we have come to despise those around
us, looking on them as tools to be used for our own
advantage. Now we come to appreciate their kindness
and compassion for us in our sufferings — their selflessness and devotion to duty. Our daily lives may
have been full of external activity — so full that we
may have found little or no time for serious thought
about spiritual things. Now we have time forced upon
us, and slowly but surely our thoughts will turn to
God. An illness can often prove to be the most effective form of a retreat from this point of view. Those
hurried confessions of the past are now replaced by
careful examinations of conscience and a realization
of the meaning of sin. We have plenty of time now
for preparation before our Holy Communions and
for a good thanksgiving afterward.

Like a hurt child who runs to his mother for relief,
we are slowly forced back to God. In that intimate

contact with Him, we shall find love, and, through that love, the mystery of pain will find its true explanation. In the end we shall discover that His yoke is sweet and that His burden is light.

Chapter Seven
∞

*Anointing of the Sick
will bring you peace
and consolation*

When we think of the importance of suffering, and especially when we realize how necessary it is for us to die well, many of us have the feeling that we shall never be able to rise to the occasion. We have been so occupied in the past with the good things of this world that we have neglected God. Shall we ever be able to accept suffering and death when the time comes? Above all, perhaps, the thought of our past life with its tale of repeated infidelities to grace makes us afraid of the very thought of death. Will even our sufferings enable us to face our Judge with anything like tranquillity?

God, in His wisdom and mercy, has foreseen all these difficulties and has provided for them. He has given us a special sacrament which will help us to prepare to meet Him face-to-face, a sacrament which will heal all the wounds of our soul and which may even heal our stricken body if it be His will. It is known as the Anointing of the Sick. We remember what St. James says about this sacrament: "Is any man sick among you? Let him bring in the priests of the Church, and let them pray over him, anointing him with oil in the name of the Lord. And the prayer of faith shall save the sick man. And the Lord shall raise him up; and if he be in sins, they shall be forgiven him."[46] But we have probably never meditated on those words with a view to finding out exactly what this sacrament is intended to do in the soul and body of the sick person.

Like all the other sacraments, the Anointing of the Sick increases the grace of God in our souls and also gives us special graces which are designed to overcome all the difficulties which sickness brings with it. We shall understand these effects better if we consider

[46] James 5:14-15.

first of all the sacrament itself and the method of administering it.

Often this sacrament is received in conjunction with Confession and Viaticum.[47] First, the priest may ask God's blessing on the house and on those present. A penitential rite follows, in which the *Confiteor*[48] may be recited, and an appropriate scriptural passage is read. Then, following a short litany, the priest lays his hands on the head of the sick person. The priest says a prayer of thanksgiving over oil specially blessed for this sacrament and anoints the forehead and hands of the sick person with it. Afterward he prays that God may restore the sick person to perfect health of soul and body, that his sins may be forgiven him, and that he may be restored once more to his family and to the Church of God. Such, in brief, is the rite of

[47] Viaticum is Holy Communion given to those in danger of death.

[48] The *Confiteor* is the penitential prayer that begins with the words "I confess."

administration. It is both simple and direct, as you can see. Now let us consider more in detail the graces which it bestows.

∞

Anointing calms and consoles

Like the other sacraments, the Anointing of the Sick gives us an increase of sanctifying grace, which means far more than mere words can adequately express. Grace is the true life of the soul, and therefore an increase in grace means an increase in life. This alone must be a great consolation to one who is facing bodily death. While the earthly life is drawing slowly to its close, the heavenly life is being steadily increased with every labored breath. God's presence is making itself ever more felt, until we can truly say with St. Paul that it is no longer we who live, but Christ who lives in us.[49] An increase in sanctifying grace means an increase in our ability to see things from God's

[49] Cf. Gal. 2:20.

point of view, from the viewpoint of eternity rather than from that of time. In this way, we learn to embrace the divine will in all things, accepting even death because it is God's will for us.

But perhaps it is in the special sacramental graces that the sick person finds most consolation. Once this sacrament has been received, a great peace descends on the soul, and with reason. If we remember the causes of our fears in danger of death, we see clearly how this peace of soul is accomplished.

The Anointing of the Sick removes all fear of the judgment which awaits the soul, because it forgives all sins, provided we are sorry for them. It can even reach beyond the limits of absolution in certain circumstances. The sick person may be unconscious, for example, yet in the depths of his soul, there is sorrow for the sins which have been committed. Absolution may not avail in this case, because the acts of the penitent cannot be expressed externally. The Anointing of the Sick forgives those sins completely.

∽

Anointing restores spiritual health

In all of us, sin dies hard; it leaves its roots in bad habits and evil inclinations, even when the guilt of sin has been removed by a good confession. The soul remains weak, just as the body does after a serious illness. One of the effects of this sacrament is to remove this weakness, bringing the soul back to perfect spiritual health. Small wonder, then, that St. Thomas Aquinas claims that this sacrament is the immediate preparation of the soul for entrance into Heaven.[50] Once it has been received with the proper dispositions, there is no longer need for us to fear the past or the judgment. In itself this is sufficient to bring great peace to the soul and to enable it to defeat all the temptations to despair which come from the Devil.

[50] Cf. St. Thomas Aquinas (1184-1225; Dominican philosopher and theologian), *Summa Theologica*, Suppl., Q. 29, art. 1.

Nor are these dispositions difficult to acquire. A good confession will produce most of them at once. If the sick person is unconscious, a habitual sorrow for sin, even if it is from the lowest motive of fear of divine punishment, is sufficient. There should also be a willingness to accept God's will; this can easily be obtained through a careful recitation of the Our Father, in which we pray that God's will may "be done on earth as it is in Heaven."

However, we have not exhausted all the possibilities of this great sacrament. It has another effect, conditioned on God's will, it is true, but nevertheless possible in every case — namely, the restoration of health if God sees it expedient. Every priest has seen instances in which the Anointing of the Sick has been responsible for complete recovery where medical science has been powerless. It is, in every sense, the sacrament of hope.

For this reason, and for many others, its reception should not be delayed until the last possible moment, when the patient has lost consciousness and there is nothing more that human science can do. On the contrary, Catholics should have a great desire to receive it at the earliest possible moment in case of serious illness, because it will help the ordinary human aids to health to attain their full effect.

Like all the sacraments, however, it produces greater effects when the personal dispositions are more perfect. Therefore, it is worthwhile to consider for a moment some simple methods of preparation for its reception. Here it would be difficult to improve on the classical catechism approach toward the problem of sorrow for sin. We are told to consider three things in order to produce that sorrow: the punishment due to sin, the death of our Lord on the Cross, and the fact that our sins are offenses against the God of love, who is also the Supreme Being.

∞

Pondering God's justice can help you avoid sin

Sin is an offense against God, and we are all aware of that, however dead our consciences may be. An offense demands justice. We have broken the law, and we must pay the price of our infidelity. In the case of grievous sin which has not yet been forgiven, that price is a very high one — the loss of Heaven for all eternity.

Think of what that means. Man is made for happiness, and if, at the end of this life, he loses Heaven, his fate is simply unhappiness forever. Surely no created thing, however attractive, is worth that! Faced with life, a man may waver in his choice between the creature and God, between temporal happiness and eternal — but faced with death, it is a different picture. Now we must leave all created things behind us, and they will never mean the same to us again. Some of them will soon be held in higher esteem, while others — the objects of our sins — will be seen in their true proportions as things which have separated us from our eternal good.

We can make a supreme effort now to break the bonds of sin once and for all. God does not mind if

this victory comes at the very last moment — quite
the contrary. His grace has been with us all the time
to achieve that end. We need have no fear. If we only
take one step toward Him, He will do the rest. He
will purify our motives and will lift up our weakness
to the heights of His divine love. With His help, there
is nothing we cannot do and no obstacle we cannot
overcome. All He asks is our willingness to cooperate
with His grace. That is surely not too much to ask.

A crucifix can move you to sorrow for sin

Take a crucifix into your hands for a moment, and
look at it carefully. There is the proof that God loves
all men with a love which far surpasses anything we
could ever imagine or hope for. As St. John Chrysostom
says, the soul of a man is so precious in God's sight
that He was willing to give His only Son in order to
win for that soul salvation.[51] If our sins have been

---

[51] Cf. St. John Chrysostom (c. 347-407; Bishop of
Constantinople), *Sermon 2 on Genesis*, sect. 1.

great, God's love has been greater. Those sins are all paid for — and more than paid for — by the death of Christ on the Cross. Can we refuse our love to One who has done so much for us?

When He died, He had me in His thoughts. He knew me intimately — all the circumstances of my life, including my sins, were before His eyes. That supreme sacrifice of His death was offered for me, that I might win eternal life and happiness with Him forever. Am I going to allow that act of love to become an empty gesture? He loved me so much that He was willing to die for me. Can I refuse to be sorry for my sins because they have been an offense against His love and the cause of His death?

If we should always keep a crucifix near us to remind us of our debt to Him, this is even more true when we are in danger of death and when the Devil is liable to tempt us to thoughts of despair. The proof of Christ's love is there for all to see. If I deny that He loves me, then the sight of His image on the Cross will give the lie to all my doubts and fears. He who never rejected a sinner during His life on earth will not reject me. In a sense, the greater my sins, the more eager will be the efforts of that love to win me over to Him at last. He is Jesus Christ, yesterday, today, and the same forever.[52]

You must be sorry for having offended God

Such thoughts as these should prepare us to rise to the very heights of sorrow. However vague our ideas of God may be, we do know that He is the Supreme Being, the Lord of creation in every sense of the word. All that we have comes from God. The whole of nature obeys Him perfectly. Only man has the terrible responsibility of being able to say no to God's law. Our sins have been offenses against God's absolute supremacy. We have set our wills against His.

Think for a moment of what that means. God is everything, while we are nothing except what God

---

[52] Cf. Heb. 13:8.

has chosen to make us. There is nothing we have which we can call our own except sin. Yet, by our sins, we have dared to set our nothingness up against His supremacy, thus bringing about a revolt in the order of nature, the like of which it would be difficult to imagine.

It should now be possible for us to throw ourselves on His mercy and confide in His love. Here our very nothingness will help us. The fact that we are helpless without Him should drive us to our knees in humble sorrow for our revolt. We can tell Him that we desire to love Him above all things, that our revolt has been thoughtless and stupid, that we are sorry for what has been wrong in our lives, and that, now at least, we are resolved to keep His law for the future.

This supreme motive for sorrow often appears rather weak to some people. Obviously, it is easier in many ways for us to concentrate on God's goodness to us, on His love for His creatures, and on the punishment we have deserved for our sins. All these thoughts bring us great consolation from the human point of view, more so, perhaps, than the thought of God's supremacy. Here we should not deceive ourselves. Those former motives for sorrow are true, useful, and sincere, of course; but this last motive is in many ways the most efficacious. Once we can bring ourselves to realize what God's supremacy means, we shall have a motive for repentance which will outdistance all the others.

The idea behind the creation of the world is that every creature should give honor and glory to God by being what God wills it to be. A tree gives honor and glory to God just by being a tree — by its growth during the various seasons of the year, by its foliage and its fruit. The same is true of the whole of nature. What is more, the tree gives glory to God by being the kind of tree it is, with all its individual characteristics.

That was also God's plan for us, and the circumstances of our lives were really just means to the realization of that plan. However, we revolted. We did not want to be formed according to His plan, but according to our own. We thought we knew better than God what was good for us and what would lead to our future happiness. So we turned away from God's plan and tried to follow our own.

Now is the moment for us to repent for having turned away. It is not too late, because He can put us back on the right road in a moment. There is plenty of room in God's plan for the Magdalenes of this world and for the Augustines.[53] All the evil effects of our revolt can be undone once we recognize God's supremacy and accept it with all our hearts, sorry for having allowed ourselves to stray from His paths.

Above all, there is one thing we can do to prove to God that we have at last decided to put ourselves under His rule in all things: we can accept death at

[53] St. Mary Magdalene (cf. Mark 16:9), often associated with the sinner who anointed Christ (Luke 7:37-38), and St. Augustine (354-430), Bishop of Hippo, are examples of penitent sinners who have risen to sainthood. — ED.

Comfort for the Sick and Dying

His hands as part of the price we have to pay for having sinned against Him. We can accept our illness in a spirit of humility, knowing that, in God's hands, it can prove an effective purification and preparation for Heaven. This will not be easy at first, because nature rebels against both sickness and death, but we can do it, provided we are careful to consider all the motives we have for accepting God's will.

Once we have managed to produce in our souls this sorrow for past sin — encompassing everything which has been an offense against God — and once we have achieved a voluntary acceptance of God's will for us, we can be sure that we are perfectly prepared to receive the Anointing of the Sick. We shall then obtain the full benefit of that great sacrament and be in a fit state to meet God face-to-face.

Fear will then give place to a great joy and peace, because we shall know that, whatever our lives may have been in the past, all is forgiven and we can now make a fresh start. The fact that our fresh start happens to coincide with the end of our lives on earth does not worry God one bit, because He looks at these things from the viewpoint of eternity, not from that of time. Besides, He sent His Son on this earth, not to call the just, but sinners.[54] Once we have received this sacrament, we can die in peace.

[54] Matt. 9:13.

Chapter Eight
∞

*How you should pray
when you are sick*

∽

This subject requires a special chapter because of its difficulty. We all know that, even at the best of times, it is not an easy thing to pray well, because so many factors enter into the exercise of prayer. Besides, we are all rather diffident about our efforts in this field — at least, if we have true humility. Yet, prayer should be as natural to us as breathing, since it is merely voluntary contact between ourselves and God. As the catechism tells us, it is the raising of our minds and hearts to God, and when we remember how much we depend on Him for all that we have, it should not be difficult to achieve such contact with Him.

In some cases, of course, prayer is hard because we have never really tried to pray. In other instances, the fact that we are not satisfied with our prayer comes from pride or from confusing prayer as such with methods of prayer or even with prayers in the plural. All these difficulties are increased rather than diminished in times of sickness or pain, when we have the added bodily incapacity to cope with, as well as all the other hindering factors.

If we are going to pray well, we must first have a clear idea of what prayer really is. In many ways, it is easier to acquire this idea if we begin by saying what prayer is not. Many words do not make a good prayer — we have our Lord's own statement for that fact.[55] Therefore, to pray well, we do not need to multiply the number of our prayers. Again, prayer is not confined to any definite method. It can be vocal — that is, said with the lips — or it can be mental — thoughts and aspirations which do not need words. It may even be the prayer of the hands or the feet — the prayer of the scrub brush, the typewriter, or the pen.

[55] Matt. 6:7.

In truth, prayer is both a state of mind and an action. Perhaps it would be better to say that prayer is an action which is intended to bring about a certain state of mind.

You must have the proper motive for prayer

To see what this means, we must examine more in detail the motives for prayer and its chief aims. Prayer should be the natural expression of our entire dependence on God. It is a voluntary contact with God, the Supreme Being, in the course of which we acknowledge His supremacy, thank Him for all His benefits, both natural and supernatural, express our sorrow for the offenses which have outraged His majesty, and also tell Him our needs, both spiritual and temporal. We pray, therefore, because it is our duty — not necessarily because we like it.

Nor do we pray so that we may change the will of God or the decrees of His Providence. Rather, we pray so that we may have the grace to do His will in all things. In the order of His Providence, God has conditioned many of His graces on our prayers for them. Therefore, because we are fully aware that all the good we have comes from God and that, left to our own efforts, we can do nothing, we pray to Him to be merciful and, in His goodness, to help us. By prayer we draw closer to God at every moment, because we realize more fully as we pray that we depend entirely on Him. By prayer our faith is increased and preserved against the temptations of the Devil, our hope finds new grounds for trusting in God, who loves us so much, and our own love for God is increased.

If prayer is necessary for all, it is even more essential when we are faced with illness and with the danger of death. All our happiness may depend on how we perform this duty now. Therefore, after considering the general conditions which make prayer efficacious, we shall pay special attention to prayer in times of illness.

The Church teaches us that, while it is right and proper to put forward our material needs to God in prayer, such material things should be asked for only insofar as they conduce to our eternal salvation. Our Lord has told us, "Seek ye first the kingdom of God and His justice, and all these things shall be added unto you."[56] That is God's approach to life seen as it should be in the light of eternity and of divine love. Can we not accept His word for it that we need not be overanxious about material things? He knows that we need them from time to time or that we are worried about them, but if we had that faith which He compared to a grain of mustard seed,[57] we would be willing to leave all these matters in His hands. In many cases, this attitude would bring quicker results.

You must be humble and persevering in prayer

Our best prayer, in the sense of the one which most easily possesses the qualities necessary to make it

[56] Matt. 6:33.
[57] Matt. 17:19.

effective, is that of submission to His divine will and a petition for the strength necessary to accept that will in our lives. Such a prayer will never fail to have its effect. We should not ask for graces which will do away with all difficulties — miraculous graces which would carry us through as they did St. Paul. In fact, it is when we ask for such graces that we are liable to become disappointed, because our prayers are not answered. We should ask for the grace to walk, not the grace to fly. As St. Francis de Sales has put it, we must desire our salvation and pray for it, but after the manner in which God has willed it, not according to some plan of our own.[58]

For this we need humility in prayer — the humility of the publican in the Gospel story.[59] As St. Augustine

---

[58] St. Francis de Sales (1567-1622; Bishop of Geneva), *Treatise on the Love of God,* Bk. 8, ch. 4. See also St. Francis de Sales, *Finding God's Will for You* (Manchester, New Hampshire: Sophia Institute Press, 1998), 17. — ED.

[59] Luke 18:10-14.

says, we are beggars in God's sight, and we must beg
from His mercy what we cannot demand as a right.
It is this humility which makes prayer so powerful.
As Christ said, "He that humbleth himself shall be
exalted"[60] — and remember that He used the example
of the publican's prayer to prove His point. Humility
gives us the help we need to persevere in prayer when
God seems deaf to our petitions. Read the story of
the Canaanite woman once again,[61] and you will see
how pleasing this humble insistence can be in the
sight of God.

Humility, in turn, gives rise to great confidence in
the mercy and the goodness of God. Not to trust in God
in prayer would be to ignore the whole life and teachings of Christ in the Gospels. Our misery and unhappiness are a direct appeal to the merciful heart of our
Savior. How many times He has promised that in the

[60] Luke 18:14.
[61] Matt. 15:22-28.

Scriptures! "Because he hoped in me, I will deliver him. . . . He shall cry to me, and I will hear him."[62] Our Lord insists on this fact, giving the touching example of a child appealing to his father for bread. He continues: "If you, being evil, know how to give good gifts to your children, how much more will your Father who is in Heaven give good things to them that ask Him?"[63] At the Last Supper, He comes back to the same thought: "Whatsoever you ask the Father in my name, that will I do, so that the Father may be glorified in the Son. If you ask me anything in my name, that will I do."[64] "In that day, you shall ask in my name; and I say not to you that I will ask the Father for you, for the Father Himself loveth you, because you have loved me."[65] Truly, we have every reason for confidence that our humble, persevering prayer will be heard.

[62] Ps. 90:14-15 (RSV = Ps. 91:14-15).
[63] Matt. 7:9-11.
[64] John 14:13-14.
[65] John 16:26-27.

Finally, we must pay attention when we pray. Prayer is an audience with God's majesty. Therefore we must be careful to avoid voluntary distractions and to attend to what we are saying, even though we may not feel very pious during the time of prayer. Feelings do not matter. If we give God generous service, He will do the rest. At all costs, we must avoid the accusation: "This people honoreth me with their lips, but their heart is far from me."[66]

Sickness may require you to pray differently

Up to this point, we have dealt with the essential qualities of a good prayer. Now let us see how these qualities apply to prayer in times of suffering, especially physical suffering, when the fear of death is at the back of our minds all the time. At such times, prayer is even more difficult than usual, partly because the physical illness has an undoubted influence on

[66] Matt. 15:8.

our mental activities, and also because the very urgency
of the situation may make us overanxious. We know
that we should make an all-out effort now, but it is so
difficult, and we tire so easily. Add to this the activity
of the Devil, who would like to see us make no effort
at all, and you can see why prayer at such times is
hard. There are, however, certain basic principles of
the spiritual life which can put us at our ease if we
will only take the time to think about them.

First, God never demands more from us than we
can give. He is both just and merciful. If we ourselves
realize the difficulty of prayer at such times, so — more
so — does He. The secret lies in a reorientation of our
attitude toward prayer. We may not be able to say many
prayers, but that does not mean we cannot pray. As
St. Thomas Aquinas says, in his simple fashion, "Man
prays so long as he directs his whole life toward God."
In the case of serious or long-drawn-out illness, we have
a splendid opportunity of doing just that. We can direct
the whole of our life, even our death, toward God.

The illness itself, with its accompanying physical weakness, makes us realize how much we depend on God. It also helps us to see the transient nature of material things and to turn our attention to the life of the spirit, which alone endures forever. Eternity becomes more important, while time matters less than it did before.

Just as we have to readjust our attitude toward many material things, which we were able to do easily before we fell ill, but which are no longer possible for us, so, in the same way, we have to readjust our spiritual values. Before we became ill, we could go to Mass, receive Holy Communion daily, recite the Rosary or other vocal prayers with ease, and perhaps we could even read some spiritual books. Now we find many of those things impossible or extremely difficult. Formerly, we could apply our whole mind to our prayers; now we get tired, have many distractions, and discover that our physical weakness makes intensive concentration impossible.

Comfort for the Sick and Dying

Now the emphasis has shifted. Our will is the important factor. We must desire with all our heart to love God above all things, to repent more sincerely for all that has ever separated us from Him, and to unite our will with His. We must live this illness in the presence of Jesus Christ and in union with His Passion and death for our own salvation and for that of others. How are we going to achieve this? Ask God every day for the grace to know Him and to love Him better.

Although prayer may be difficult, it is still possible for us to make the short acts of faith, hope, charity, and contrition. We should say these slowly, thinking all the time of what we are saying and willing it with all our strength. With a crucifix before us, we can remind ourselves of that great act of love, be sorry for our offenses against God, and will to love Him with our whole heart. We should also make good use of brief, spontaneous prayers during illness — again making them slowly and thinking of what we are saying.

Another very useful practice in times of illness is reading the Passion of our Lord from the Gospels. If we cannot read it ourselves, perhaps someone can read it to us slowly and carefully. That story will inspire us, as nothing else can, to accept our sufferings in union with those of the Son of God. All we need to do is to tell Him several times a day that we accept willingly whatever He may send us. In particular, we accept this illness and even death itself, if it be His will for us, in union with His Passion and death on the Cross. This is a great act of virtue and brings many rewards. It should never be neglected.

When we are ill, to help us to achieve this union with Christ in His sufferings, it is a good thing to make the Stations of the Cross while looking at a crucifix. A useful prayer for this purpose is: "We adore Thee, O Christ, and we praise Thee, because by Thy holy Cross, Thou hast redeemed the world." Those who are so ill that even this effort is too much for them might look at or kiss the crucifix. The devotion of the

Stations of the Cross has such a wonderful effect in uniting us with the sufferings of our Lord that it should become a common practice when one is sick.

Apart from God Himself, there is no one who can help us so efficaciously to unite ourselves with Christ in His Passion as Mary, His Mother, who stood so heroically at the foot of the Cross, making His sacrifice her own. If we ask her help and put ourselves under her special protection, she will see to it that we accept the will of God and that we do not waste these precious moments of our pain. She will be with us at the moment of our death, and her mother's love will help us to die well. If we can, we should recite her Rosary, or at least join in while others say it with us. We can invoke her aid under those grand titles which the Church uses in her litany. We can say brief, spontaneous prayers to her from time to time.

We may not be able to go to Mass, but at least we can unite ourselves in spirit several times a day with all the Masses which are being offered at every moment of the day and night throughout the whole world. They are being offered for all, living and dead, and we shall profit by the graces they obtain from God. We can make our little acts of faith, hope, charity, and contrition in union with those sacrifices. At every moment, if we wish to do so, we can also offer our sufferings in union with those of Christ through the Mass.

Confession and Communion will console you

Our greatest consolation during sickness will be our confessions and Communions. By a careful use of these sacraments, we can purify our soul, bringing it into ever-increasing union with Christ.

Where our confessions are concerned, the important thing is sorrow for sin, together with a firm resolution to avoid it in the future. This is not difficult now, because illness does a great deal to stifle any lingering affection we may have for sin. During illness, make full use of your opportunities of going to Confession. Remember that the graces of the sacraments are specially adapted to the circumstances of life, and the grace we receive through Confession can prevent our falling into the same sins again. It will enable us to resist temptation, especially the special temptations which can come to us through our illness.

The preparation for Holy Communion should be made carefully. We might remember that we are going to receive Christ, who loves us above all things and who is longing to help us. Here is the main source of our strength to bear our illness and even death itself. If He is with us, then we can do all things and suffer all things. When He comes to us in Holy Communion, we should offer ourselves entirely to Him, tell Him of our special needs in this illness, and ask Him to prepare us fully for Heaven by removing any defects which might hinder our journey to God. During those moments after Communion, we can usually find enough courage to offer Him our lives in union with His death on the

Cross in satisfaction for our own sins and for those
of the world.

Your prayer can be efficacious even in sickness

Those who have led very active lives have a special
difficulty when a serious illness overtakes them. They
are only too ready to think that now they are useless
and a burden to others. If this thought is allowed to
take hold on them, they may rebel against their illness
and so lose many graces they might otherwise have
obtained through it.

Such people should remember that the really important thing in life is to do God's will. There is often
more truly spiritual activity on a bed of pain than there
is in the course of a whole life devoted to active work.
Often we are too busy to make time for a retreat, but an
illness often proves the best retreat we have ever made.
Above all, it brings us into contact with the greatest
of all truths: that one day we shall have to leave all
this activity in order to meet God face-to-face.

Comfort for the Sick and Dying

Since the secret of all prayer is to direct our lives toward God so that all our actions have a supernatural value, in times of sickness, we should make a special effort to do this. The morning offering of all our thoughts, words, deeds, and sufferings will fix this intention for us. That intention should be repeated several times in the course of the day, because undoubtedly the best prayer we shall ever make is this determination to live and die in union with God's will for us. We may be so ill that vocal prayer becomes almost impossible, but this prayer of action — of suffering in union with Christ — is always within our grasp. We can be quite sure that, if we use this opportunity properly, we shall never make a better or more efficacious prayer.

There is no need for us to worry, therefore, if we find that many of the types of prayer we have mentioned here are impossible for us. This prayer of being content to remain quiet, doing God's will, is always possible. Every moment, every pain, every breath is a prayer. The mind and the will can still fix their attention on God, even though our vocal prayer may have to be limited to that of Christ in His agony in the garden, and that is all that really matters. If we do the best we can, He will accept and consecrate our poor efforts, which of themselves are worthless, and will make them into a perfect prayer by uniting them with His own great prayer on the Cross: "Father, into Thy hands I commend my spirit."[67]

[67] Luke 23:46.

Chapter Nine

*How you can
resist temptation when
you are suffering*

※

The modern tendency is to scoff at all belief in the existence of the Devil, and, of course, nothing pleases him more than that. When people believe that he exists, they are liable to take precautions against his attacks. On the other hand, we must avoid going to extremes, because not all temptations come directly from the Devil; there are some which arise naturally from the varied circumstances of life and others which come from the weakness of our fallen human nature.

If this is true of the normal circumstances of life, it is still more true in time of illness, when we are not strong and every effort costs us much more than it did when we were healthy. Consequently, a word or two about the usual temptations which attack sick people, whether they come from the Devil or from circumstances, will not be out of place here. We need not mention those which have already been dealt with in previous chapters.

The rebellion of human nature against sickness is a natural reaction. Very few people really like being ill, and those who do are not normal. However, this reaction can constitute a temptation insofar as it may lead us to rebel against the will of God and refuse to accept our illness as a punishment for our sins and a means of expiation. The best method of dealing with this temptation is by the constant repetition of acts of submission to the will of God and of confidence in His goodness. God knows perfectly well that the reaction against sickness and pain is natural. He will not condemn us for having those instinctive feelings — provided we do not give in to them.

Again, we can remember that all the circumstances of our lives form part of God's plan for our salvation. They are permitted and directed by One who loves us more than we can ever imagine. We can always trust ourselves with complete confidence to His loving care, safe in the knowledge that there is a purpose behind our pain, even though we may not be able to see very clearly what it is. In general terms, we know that nothing makes us so much like Christ as suffering which is willingly accepted in union with His Passion. There is great consolation in that thought if we meditate upon it. Suffering is the royal road which leads to Heaven.

Another natural reaction to suffering is the feeling of loneliness which it sometimes brings with it. This is especially true of those who have to spend a great deal of their time of sickness in hospitals or other institutions. Visitors are not too frequent, we miss the loving care of our family, and the circumstances of hospital routine leave us with a sense of isolation.

This same feeling is not uncommon among those who are ill in their own homes. We feel that those around us are powerless to help, however kind and considerate they may be. There is the conviction that no one really understands what suffering this illness implies in our case.

There is a feeling of helplessness and inevitability about the whole thing which can make the sick feel very lonely at times. Sickness is a world of its own which those who are healthy find it difficult to understand. Time drags on very slowly and painfully, while sometimes even sleep is impossible.

Undoubtedly, this is a very real suffering added to the purely physical pain of illness, especially if it be a long one. How are we to deal with it? Once again, the thought of Christ in His Passion will help us. He knew before He began to suffer that He would have to go through with it alone. He warned the Apostles that they would all run away and leave Him to His fate.[68] During most of His Passion He was surrounded, not by loving friends who would at least try to console Him, but by His bitter enemies who would not even allow

[68] Cf. Matt. 26:56.

Him to die in peace. At one moment, it seemed that
His Father in Heaven had also deserted Him in that
hour of trial.[69]

∞

You are never alone in your suffering

Our illness is not really like that, because He who
understands so well what it meant to feel lonely is
with us. We are the branches of the True Vine, the
members of His Mystical Body, one with Him in some
mysterious fashion. We can never be alone, much less
when, like Him, we are stretched on the Cross of pain.
He will never leave us during those moments.

His Mother will be with us too. Like her Son, she
understands what it means to suffer — and she is our
mother also. She knows how very important it is that
we should be like her Son, and He gave us into her
charge at that solemn moment of His death on the
Cross. Her task is not finished until we reach Heaven,

[69] Cf. Matt. 27:46.

for she has a special interest in our salvation. More tenderly than any earthly mother, she will care for us and console us, never leaving us until she can deliver our souls into the hands of her Son.

The prayers of the whole Church are with us all our lives, but especially when we are suffering. We are all one in Christ, our Head, and that solidarity means that we can never be alone. Our pain is a very real part of the Church's redemptive mission in the world; it is a continuation of the pain of Christ, and, when our pain is united with that Passion, it is Christ Himself who suffers in and with us for the Church. We have the whole army of the saints in Heaven on our side, together with the intercession of the souls in Purgatory. There is also the whole of the Church on earth to call on when we need help. We can never be alone.

Our guardian angel will be watching over us, because he knows how difficult it can be for us to suffer, especially to make the most of suffering from the spiritual point of view. He realizes the purifying effect pain can have on the soul — how it can draw us ever nearer to Christ and purge away the last remnants of sin or of the debt of temporal punishment we owe for the past. Like God Himself, our guardian angel would rather see us suffer a little here than expiate our sins in Purgatory. He wants us to go straight to Heaven when we die. Therefore he guards us carefully against the last furious attacks of the Devil and helps us to turn our very temptations into occasions of great merit.

The solitude of illness, then, is only apparent. We are not really alone. However, there is yet another method of dealing with this temptation. We can call upon the Holy Spirit, who has been given to us in a special way in Confirmation, asking Him to increase our fortitude, to give us courage to accept even this feeling of loneliness in union with the will of God. Under His guidance and by His grace, we shall be willing to strip ourselves of all human consolations in order to receive those of God Himself — that peace which the world cannot give.[70]

∞

You must beware temptations to despair

As we might expect, the Devil reserves some special temptations for those who are seriously ill, and although there is no need for us to fear him unduly, still it is a good thing to know his usual methods of attack and how we can turn them to our own advantage.

By the thought of our past sins or even through the physical pain of our illness, he may tempt us to despair — a sin which can take many forms, including the attitude which denies any meaning to life and thus destroys the whole purpose of God's grace. Naturally, our past sins now appear in their true light, without that cloak of attraction they wore at the time when we committed them. We realize now how futile they were and how incapable of giving us that happiness we sought

[70] John 14:27.

in them. The Devil sometimes makes use of these thoughts and may cause us to worry about our past confessions, the sincerity of our sorrow, or our determination to amend our ways. Have we really been forgiven for all that has been wrong in our lives? In this and in many other ways, the Devil tries his best to disturb our peace of mind — in a word, to withdraw our thoughts from God and fasten them once again upon ourselves.

The perfect, all-satisfying answer to these temptations is, of course, the sacrament of Anointing. Against that weapon, the Devil is powerless to harm us. He is like a chained dog who cannot bite us unless we put ourselves within his reach.[71] However, we must learn to use the graces of this sacrament to the full.

∞

You must trust in God's promises

The defense against the temptation to despair is the virtue of hope, together with our faith in God.

[71] Cf. St. John Vianney (1786-1859; patron saint of parish priests), *Sermon on Temptations*.

Comfort for the Sick and Dying

Remember His love and His promises. No one who comes to Him will ever be cast out — even if he comes at the last moment. He loves us far more than He hates our sins, and if we are sorry for them, He will forgive us. Christ's mission on earth was directed especially toward sinners, and His expiation on the Cross was accomplished for their sakes. The grace which was strong enough to convert St. Peter after his denial of our Lord and to convert St. Augustine, Mary Magdalene, and Margaret of Cortona[72] after many years of sin is also strong enough for us.

Our task in this life — and in many ways, it is our supreme trial — is to journey toward God by faith. We do not see clearly in this world; we have to believe God's word and have confidence in His promises and in His love. If we only realized it, this is our great safeguard, because if we deal with God in utter simplicity

[72] Margaret of Cortona (died 1297), penitent sinner who became a Third Order Franciscan; known as the "Magdalene of the Seraphic Order."

and confidence, as a child would deal with his father, there can be no doubt at all about the result. Only a madman would abuse the trusting confidence of a child.

Above all, God asks this of us: that we trust Him. And He has given us every reason for doing so. We should not allow anything to disturb the serenity of this faith and confidence. We know that He desires our salvation even more than we do. Therefore, having done our best to put right the mistakes of the past, we can safely leave the rest to Him.

So far as past confessions are concerned, unless we have some good and positive reasons for doubting them, we must learn not to worry. Here, our present confessions can help us. If we are really worried about something in the past, we can mention it to a priest again now and ask his help. Our present sorrow can make up for past deficiencies, and at least now we can have a firm resolution to avoid all sin for the future. In moments of worry or temptation, a slow repetition of

the acts of faith, hope, charity, and contrition, together with a little prayer to our Lady, will usually be
sufficient to remove the difficulty and to make these
moments occasions of greater confidence in God.

You must resist spiritual indifference

There is another temptation which cannot be
passed over in silence. It is the inclination to be indif-
ferent about spiritual matters which sometimes accom-
panies grave illness. We feel that we have come to the
end of our tether, both physically and spiritually, and
that nothing really matters anymore. We are quite satisfied, perhaps, with the very little we give to God and
do not make much effort to improve our prayers, confessions, and Communions. At times, this has a com-
panion thought with it: a sense of complete failure.
We feel that life has been useless and without purpose.
The danger of this temptation is increased, if at the
same time, we begin to worry about our material obligations, or our husband, wife, or children. We may be

so concerned with these material things that we do not give sufficient time to our spiritual welfare.

It is natural that our family obligations should concern us during illness, especially if there is danger of death. However, once again we must learn to trust in the God who told us that we are of much more value than the birds of the air and the flowers of the field.[73] We can safely confide those obligations into God's hands, because He knows and loves our family even more than we do. He will see to it that no real harm comes to them if and when they should be deprived of our help. We have one supreme task at the moment, and we must see to it that it is well done. If it is God's will that we should die as a result of this illness, we must accept that will and prepare for death. That is our first and most important obligation, and we can begin to think of the others when we have carried out this one.

[73] Cf. Matt. 6:26, 30.

Comfort for the Sick and Dying

Many people come to the end of their lives feeling that they have failed. Remember that no one who reaches Heaven has failed, because that is the only success which really counts. However, we may have failed in the material things of life, the final success is always open to us until the very last moment. From the human standpoint, Christ's life was a failure: His followers had all deserted Him, and He was put to death like a common criminal. But from God's point of view, it was the outstanding triumph of history. Our lives can be a reflection of that supreme triumph if we care to make them so.

We must never allow the spirit of indifference to overcome us. Here, a supreme effort is sometimes needed in order to force ourselves to take an active part in our own salvation. Above all, there must be an effort to pray. We must do everything we can to receive the sacraments in the proper dispositions, making careful preparation for Confession and a good thanksgiving after Holy Communion. We must try to

see the grave spiritual implications of our sickness,
the possibility of death, and the responsibility of dying
well. This is our great chance, and we must grasp it at
all costs.

You must be patient with those who care for you

It would be impossible to speak about all the minor
temptations which come to us through illness. However, we may be forgiven for returning to one which
has already been mentioned before — namely, the
temptation to impatience. Instead of remaining qui-
etly under God's care, content to do His will, there
is a natural tendency to see the end of our illness one
way or the other. People bother us, too, because they
do not seem to realize our needs. Little things can
assume undue proportions when we are sick. We may
even make great demands on those around us almost
without realizing that we are doing so, and often these
demands are more than the situation really warrants.
Sick people can be very exacting. They can also

develop an exaggerated sympathy for themselves in their present situation.

These temptations are worth resisting, because if we overcome them, we shall be more purified and stripped of earthly things than we were before. Consequently, we shall be more ready to meet God face-to-face. Again, the secret lies in a studied imitation of Christ, our model. He did not complain during His Passion, nor did He demand anything — yet He was the Son of God made man. Learn to be patient, then, as He was.

Accept with gratitude the administrations of others, however rough they may be at times, because these small sacrifices have a great value at this stage — greater than they appear to have, perhaps. Those around you are doing their best, and you must try to show them due gratitude. Don't demand too much from them. Remember that you cannot expect them to realize fully what it means to be unable to do things for oneself. Above all, don't hurt them by anything you say. Remember that your unkind words may last in their memories for a long time and may bring them sorrow long after you are dead.

In general, be very open with the priest when he comes to visit you. He expects you to talk to him about spiritual things and will not be surprised if you mention your worries to him. If you are afraid to talk about them in general conversation, at least you can mention them when you go to Confession. The priest is there in the place of Christ and with His divine authority. He will be able to guide your conscience through all its difficulties.

Temptations can be occasions of grace

There is never any need for us to fear temptation, provided we do not thrust ourselves into it. On the contrary, God allows His faithful servants to be tempted in order to make them more anxious to turn to Him for help. It is one of the many ways in which we come to realize how much we depend on Christ and how little we can do to help ourselves. Also, temptation can be an occasion of much grace to us if we use it in the right way. It can become something meritorious, and, as such, is of great value in the struggle toward Heaven. The fight against these trials is sometimes hard and long, but it is well worth the effort. "My grace is sufficient for thee," our Lord told St. Paul.[74] The same is true in our case. We can do all things if we remain in union with Christ.

[74] 2 Cor. 12:9.

Chapter Ten
∽

*Death will perfect
your union with God*

∞

In a letter written about his father's death, Pascal[75]
says, "Let us not grieve like pagans who have no hope.
We did not lose our father at the moment of his death;
we lost him, as it were, when he entered the Church
by Baptism. From that day on, he belonged to God;
his life was vowed to God. All his actions were concerned with this life only for the sake of God. At his
death, he separated himself completely from his sins,
and now he is received by God and his sacrifice is accomplished and crowned. Thus he performed what he
vowed. He has finished the work God assigned to him.
He has achieved the only thing for which he was
created."

[75] Blaise Pascal (1623-1662), French theologian and
mathematician.

That letter sums up admirably the Christian attitude toward death. It is the last stage of a journey —
the culmination of a life dedicated to the service of
God at the moment of Baptism. The full perfection
of the union with Christ which was begun in our souls
by Baptism and continued by the other sacraments has
now been attained. It is important to see this purpose
of the sacraments clearly if we are to understand and
accept death.

∞

The sacraments prepare you for Heaven

The redemptive power of Christ comes into contact with the soul through the sacraments and steadily
transforms it into another Christ. Baptism gives us the
life of Christ for the first time; we are born again to a
new dignity, that of sons of God with the right to call
Him our Father. The Trinity dwells within us, and our
destiny is Heaven with God for eternity.

Confirmation brings that new life to maturity.
Once we have received it, we are no longer infants,

but grown men and women spiritually, with a mission in life. That mission is our own perfection and the salvation of others by our example as soldiers of Christ.

If sin should enter the realms of grace and tend to break the bond which unites us with Christ, His redemptive power is at hand once again in the sacrament of Penance. One really sincere confession with a deep sorrow arising from love can convert the sinner into a saint in a moment, so great is the power of Christ's Redemption. In this sacrament, we also share in His expiation, since it is by His merits that our souls are healed of their wounds. Penance should lead us a step farther on our journey by joining us even more intimately with our Redeemer.

When we consider the Holy Eucharist, we are at the very heart of this mystery of union with Christ. He gave us this great gift because, when people are in love, they tend naturally to live together. He loves us so much that He longs to be with us always. He comes to us in Holy Communion to be the life and food of our souls. "He that eateth me . . . shall live by me."[76] He gives us the Mass in order that, in union with Him, we may be able to fulfill perfectly our obligations of adoring, thanking, and petitioning God for all our needs. Here we have a personal sacrifice of expiation for our sins, as well as a source of grace which is nothing less than the Cross itself.

In Holy Orders, He consecrates "other Christs" to His service, giving us priests who can teach, bless, sacrifice, and forgive in His name.

In Matrimony, He gives people the grace to save their souls by a mutual life together, lived in union with Him. They are now "two in one flesh,"[77] and we should never forget that their mutual love is a living symbol of the union of Christ with His Church — that is, with us.

[76] John 6:58.
[77] Eph. 5:31.

Every stage of our life has been consecrated to
God by the sacraments, and the last step from this
world into the next has not been forgotten.

The Anointing of the Sick is, in some ways, the
greatest demonstration of the divine love and mercy.
As St. Thomas says, a soul that has received this sacrament in the right dispositions should be perfectly prepared for entry into Heaven. Sin has been removed
from the soul, doubts and fears are banished, and the
evil effects of sin are wiped away. God now reigns
supreme. Where, before, all might have been turmoil
and worry, now there is perfect peace. The Devil is
chained so that he cannot harm the soul, and his
temptations serve only as instruments of merit. Holy
Communion under the form of Viaticum — provision
for the journey — strengthens the soul still further
and makes its union with our Lord more intimate.

We are now truly sons of God, returning home
after a long and sometimes very painful journey. In
a very short while, the task we undertook at Baptism

will be completed. Well may our Lord say to us, in the words of the poet, "All which thy child's mistake fancies as lost, I have stored for thee at home / Rise, clasp my hand, and come."

At this moment, there is one last act of our will which can and should complete the union between us and Christ: the willing acceptance of death in loving faith. This act of heroic virtue will purify us from the temporal punishment which may yet remain to be suffered for past sin. It is such a supreme act of faith and confidence in God's promises and love that He, on His part, will respond to it with His usual generosity. We can give our souls into God's hands without fear of the future.

It need not surprise us, therefore, to discover that, in the New Testament, death is spoken of as a conquest, not as a failure. Again, this is due to our union with Christ, our Head, who Himself overcame death as we shall overcome it. "I am the resurrection and the life: he that believeth in me, though he be dead, shall live; and everyone that liveth and believeth in me shall not die forever."[78] Death came into the world through sin, but Christ, who redeemed us from sin, has indeed robbed death of its sting.

In her prayers for the dying, the Church has no hesitation in saying, "Go forth, O Christian soul, out of this world, in the name of God the Father almighty who created thee; in the name of Jesus Christ, the Son of the living God, who suffered for thee; in the name of the Holy Spirit, who sanctified thee." We have no need to be afraid of death, therefore, if we have this attitude toward it and prepare for it in this spirit.

∞

Death will carry you home to God

We are going home, where we really belong. There we shall find peace from all the trials and sufferings we have had to endure during this mortal life. Christ

[78] John 11:25-26.

Himself promised that He was leaving this world only in order to prepare a place for us in that other life where God Himself shall be our prize and our consolation. As St. John says, speaking of the blessed in Heaven: "And God himself . . . shall be their God. And God shall wipe away all tears from their eyes; and death shall be no more, nor mourning, nor crying, nor sorrow shall be any more, for the former things are passed away."[79] That is the glory which awaits us after death — a glory and happiness which it is beyond the heart of man to conceive.

You can see why it is so important to see these things in their right proportions now. After death, it will be too late. St. Francis de Sales sums it up in these words: "How soon we shall be in eternity. There we shall know how little it has to do with the affairs of this world, and how little it matters if we have succeeded in them or not. Yet how we bother about them

[79] Rev. 21:3-4.

as if they were so important! When we were little children, how busy we were in collecting pieces of brick, wood, and mud to make a little house or hut. And how we would have wept if someone had broken it down! But now we know very well that all this was of no importance. The same will come to pass in Heaven, when we know that all the troubles of this world were in reality only childish matters. . . . When the evening comes which brings us rest — that is, when death approaches — the little house does not matter at all, because we must enter the house of our Father. So attend faithfully to your affairs, but be assured that there is no affair so important as your eternal salvation, and that nothing is so important for your salvation as keeping your soul on the path that leads to true happiness in God."[80]

[80] Letter 455 to Madame de la Flérchère, May 19, 1608; see St. Francis de Sales, *Thy Will Be Done* (Manchester, New Hampshire: Sophia Institute Press, 1995), 48-49. — ED.

Comfort for the Sick and Dying

∞

You will rise again in glory

And the body is not entirely forgotten in this hour of our triumph. It is true that we shall be separated from it for a time, but it is also true that one day our bodies will once again rise from the dust to share our glory in Heaven. The Resurrection of Christ, that ultimate triumph of the Cross, will be perpetuated and continued in the resurrection of the dead. He came to make full reparation for the sin of Adam, to restore everything that we lost through Adam, and to conquer sin in all its consequences. He will leave nothing whatever to the power of Satan. In and through Christ, the complete man was redeemed, both soul and body, flesh and spirit. He has already raised our souls to life through Baptism, and on the last day, He will also raise our bodies.

St. Paul describes this resurrection. The body which is sown in corruption shall rise incorruptible; from dishonor it shall pass to glory, from weakness to power. It dies a natural body; it shall rise a spiritual body. When that great moment comes, the final victory over death will have been accomplished. "And when this mortal hath put on immortality, then shall come to pass the saying which is written: Death is swallowed up in victory. O Death, where is thy victory? O Death, where is thy sting?"[81]

There is no need for us to be afraid of death if we are prepared for it, because Christ has destroyed its power to harm us, and our death has been, as it were, consecrated in His death on the Cross. God sees in our death the image of the death of His Son, with whom we are one. It still comes as a consequence of sin, but now, after Christ's death and Resurrection, it also serves as a channel of grace. For the Catholic who dies after a careful preparation, death can truly be called a glorious adventure.

[81] 1 Cor. 15:42-44, 54-55.

Sophia Institute Press®

∞

Sophia Institute is a nonprofit institution that seeks to restore man's knowledge of eternal truth, including man's knowledge of his own nature, his relation to other persons, and his relation to God. Sophia Institute Press® serves this end in numerous ways: it publishes translations of foreign works to make them accessible for the first time to English-speaking readers; it brings out-of-print books back into print; and it publishes important new books that fulfill the ideals of Sophia Institute. These books afford readers a rich source of the enduring wisdom of mankind.

Sophia Institute Press® makes these high-quality books available to the general public by using advanced technology and by soliciting donations to subsidize its general publishing costs. Your generosity can help

Sophia Institute Press® to provide the public with editions of works containing the enduring wisdom of the ages. Please send your tax-deductible contribution to the address below. We also welcome your questions, comments, and suggestions.

For your free catalog, call:
Toll-free: 1-800-888-9344

or write:
Sophia Institute Press®
Box 5284, Manchester, NH 03108

or visit our website:
www.sophiainstitute.com

Sophia Institute is a tax-exempt institution
as defined by the Internal Revenue Code,
Section 501(c)(3). Tax I.D. 22-2548708.